family baking

family baking

easy recipes for every occasion

RYLAND PETERS & SMALL
LONDON • NEW YORK

Sarah Randell

photography by Kate Whitaker

Dedication
For my parents, for teaching me what good food is all about.

Design, Photographic Art Direction and Prop Styling Steve Painter
Senior Editor Céline Hughes
Production Controller Toby Marshall
Art Director Leslie Harrington

Food Stylist Joss Herd
Food Stylist's Assistants Tim Jenner and Laura Fyfe
Indexer Hilary Bird

Originally published as 'Weekend Baking' in 2010

This revised edition published in 2013 by Ryland Peters & Small
20–21 Jockey's Fields
London WC1R 4BW
and
519 Broadway, 5th Floor
New York, NY 10012
www.rylandpeters.com

10 9 8 7 6 5 4 3 2 1

Text © Sarah Randell 2010, 2013
Design and photographs
© Ryland Peters & Small 2010, 2013

Printed in China

ISBN: 978 1 84975 427 9

A CIP record for this book is available from the British Library.

Sarah Randell began her career in private catering and as a chef before moving on to recipe writing and development for New Covent Garden Soup Co. For more than ten years, she worked with Delia Smith in the development of recipes for her magazine, television shows and 13 of her best-selling cookery books. Sarah is Food Director at *Sainsbury's Magazine*.

Author's acknowledgments
Thank you to the team at Ryland Peters & Small, plus Kate Whitaker and the lovely Joss for such gorgeous pics. And, a special thank you to B, for tasting umpteen cakes with me, both the successes and the slightly doubtful, with unfaltering enthusiasm and always, with a smile, x.

Publisher's acknowledgements
For kind loan of props:
Jane Wicks
Kitchenalia at 'Country Ways'
Strand Quay, Rye, East Sussex
Tel: 01797 227 210

Soendergaard Design for hand-thrown porcelain.
soendergaarddesign.co.uk

Kitchenaid for the loan of the electric stand mixer featured in this book. Visit www.kitchenaid.com for more of their products and your nearest stockist.

The lovely Kitty for being the perfect child model.

Nuala McArdle for hair and make-up.

Steve Painter and Nuala McArdle for allowing us to use their home in Hastings for location photography.

The original edition is cataloged as follows:
Library of Congress Cataloging-in-Publication Data

Randell, Sarah.
  Weekend baking : easy recipes for relaxed family baking / Sarah Randell ; photography by Kate Whitaker.
    p. cm.
  Includes index.
  ISBN 978-1-84975-033-2
  1. Baking. 2. Desserts. I. Title.
  TX763.R24 2010
  641.8'15--dc22
                              2010022713

Kate Whitaker has received wide recognition for her food photography. Her work has appeared in many publications, such as *Jamie magazine*, *Waitrose Food Illustrated*, *delicious* and *The Sunday Telegraph Stella* magazine. For Ryland Peters & Small she has photographed *The Guilt-free Gourmet* and *Make, Bake & Celebrate*.

Notes
• All spoon measurements are based on measuring spoons and are level unless otherwise stated.

• Butter is salted, unless otherwise stated. If you need softened butter for a recipe, leave it at room temperature for several hours before you start. I leave it out of the fridge overnight if I am using it for baking the next day.

• All baking pan measurements given are base measurements. Use non-stick bakeware to avoid sticky moments.

• All eggs are large, unless otherwise stated. If possible, use eggs at room temperature.

• I like to use unrefined sugar (such as Billington's: www.billingtons.co.uk) The flavours are more complex than refined sugars and enhance the final results. A word of warning though – unrefined icing/confectioners' sugar isn't white, so although it can look gorgeous on some cakes, it may not always be the best option to use for icings and frostings!

• Ovens should be preheated to the specified temperature. Recipes in this book were tested using a regular oven. If using a fan-assisted oven, follow the manufacturer's instructions for adjusting temperatures.

contents

Introduction

A day spent in the kitchen, mixing and baking, with the radio murmuring in the background is, to me, a day well spent. The warmth of the oven and the deliciously sweet, spicy, chocolatey or citrussy smells that may waft from its tightly closed door are not only truly comforting but ultimately satisfying too. Whether it be a batch of buttery madeleines, a tray of fruit-packed muffins, some giant chocolate chip cookies or a traditional chocolate cake for a birthday, I guarantee you will feel wonderfully smug and proud as they cool on a rack in the kitchen, waiting to be devoured or coated in a whipped icing or sticky glaze.

Children tend to be particularly enthusiastic about helping when it comes to baking. There are plenty of opportunities for little fingers to taste from the bowl, helping to mix and then to decorate and show what they have made. I'm not suggesting that children should eat cake every day, nor that we adults should, but quiet interludes in the kitchen can be just as absorbing for them as for us and highly rewarding. The time it takes to bake a cake is, in my experience, as enjoyable as eating it.

If you are a beginner, there are lots of simple baking recipes here to tempt you. All you need is some time and a few basic tools. If you are buying new tins, I urge you to invest in some good-quality kit – it really will be worth it in the long run and will last for years. As for mixing, I have an electric mixer, which I use for nearly all my baking, but I used to rely on an electric hand whisk that I have now had for 20 years and it is still going strong. If you don't have anything similar, a mixing bowl and a balloon whisk or wooden spoon, accompanied by a bit of elbow grease, will usually suffice.

For more experienced cooks, there are some new ideas here to try and have fun with. Whatever takes your fancy, I hope sugar and spice become as big a part of your storecupboard in the future as they are mine. Happy baking.

small cakes

scones with strawberry jam and plenty of clotted cream

Scones are best eaten the day they are made, but they do freeze well if you have a few left over. Another time, try adding the grated zest of a lemon and a small handful of sultanas or chopped, pitted dates to the mix.

1 large egg

about 125 ml/½ cup milk

a squeeze of lemon juice

225 g/1¾ cups plain/all-purpose flour

2 rounded teaspoons baking powder

2 tablespoons (caster) sugar, plus extra for sprinkling

a pinch of salt

50 g/3 tablespoons butter, softened and cubed

strawberry jam, to serve

clotted cream, to serve

a plain 4–5-cm/2-in. cookie cutter

a baking sheet, oiled

Makes about 10

Preheat the oven to 220°C (425°F) Gas 7.

Put the egg and milk in a small jug or bowl and lightly beat, then mix in the lemon juice.

Sift the flour and baking powder into a large mixing bowl and stir in the 2 tablespoons of sugar and the salt.

Scatter the cubes of butter over the flour mixture and, using a table knife, cut them into the flour. Now, lightly rub the butter into the flour, using your fingertips, until the mixture resembles breadcrumbs.

Pour in half the egg mixture and, using the knife again, mix the liquid into the dry ingredients using a cutting action. Add as much of the remaining egg mixture as you need to, to be able to bring everything together into a dough – you probably won't need it all.

Tip the dough out onto a lightly floured work surface and gently pat it out until it is about 2.5 cm/1 inch thick. Using the cutter, stamp out scones, then gently re-form the dough and continue until you have used it all.

Arrange the scones on the baking sheet. Brush the tops with any leftover egg mixture and sprinkle generously with (caster) sugar. Bake in the preheated oven for 10–12 minutes, or until risen and golden.

Let the scones cool on a wire rack. Serve with generous amounts of jam and clotted cream to spread on the halved scones.

toffee pear muffins

The toffee in these muffins is dulce de leche: thick, luscious Argentinian caramel, sold in tins or jars. It also makes a delicious sauce to serve with sautéed pears, apples or bananas, for a quick pudding, if you have some left over.

150 g/10 tablespoons butter

150 ml/⅔ cup milk

3 large eggs

6 tablespoons dulce de leche

100 g/½ cup packed light brown soft sugar, plus extra for sprinkling

300 g/2⅓ cups self-raising flour

1 rounded teaspoon baking powder

2 rounded teaspoons mixed/apple pie spice

2 large, ripe but firm pears, cored, peeled and chopped into small pieces

1 rounded tablespoon porridge oats

a 12-hole muffin pan, lined with muffin cases

Makes 12

Preheat the oven to 200°C (400°F) Gas 6.

Melt the butter in a small pan and let cool slightly.

In a large mixing bowl and using a balloon whisk, whisk together the milk, eggs, 2 tablespoons of the dulce de leche, the sugar and the melted butter.

Sift in the flour, baking powder and mixed/apple pie spice and whisk together. Scatter the chopped pear over the top and, using a large metal spoon, gently fold it in until just combined.

Divide the mixture (which will be quite sloppy) between the muffin cases. Sprinkle each muffin with a little extra sugar and a few porridge oats. Bake the muffins in the preheated oven for 30–35 minutes, or until risen and lightly golden.

Let the muffins cool for 10 minutes or so, then, using a small, sharp knife, cut a small cross in the top of each muffin and spoon half a teaspoonful of dulce de leche into each one. Let it settle, then add another half a teaspoonful to sit on top. Eat while still warm.

chocolate heaven muffins

These muffins are bursting with chocolate and are as easy as pie to rustle up.
For the ultimate chocolate experience, eat them fresh from the oven.

75 g/5 tablespoons butter

75 g/2½ oz. dark/bittersweet
chocolate (about 50% cocoa
solids)

75 g/2½ oz. milk chocolate

50 g/2 oz. white chocolate

100 g/½ cup sour cream

3 tablespoons milk

50 g/¼ cup light muscovado
or packed light brown soft
sugar

2 large eggs

175 g/1⅓ cups plain/
all-purpose flour

2 tablespoons cocoa powder

1 tablespoon baking powder

a pinch of salt

1 tablespoon demerara
sugar

a 6-hole muffin pan, lined
with muffin cases

Makes 6

Preheat the oven to 200°C (400°F) Gas 6.

Melt the butter in a small pan and let cool slightly.

Chop the three types of chocolate into small chunks.

In a large mixing bowl and using a balloon whisk, whisk
together the sour cream, milk, muscovado sugar, eggs
and melted butter.

Sift in the flour, cocoa and baking powder. Sprinkle in
the salt and add all the chopped chocolate. Using a
large metal spoon, fold everything together until
combined, but don't over-mix.

Divide the mixture between the muffin cases. Sprinkle
each muffin with a little demerara sugar. Bake the
muffins in the preheated oven for 20 minutes – by which
time they will be risen, but still very slightly unset in the
middle. They will continue to cook as they cool.

crunchy-topped raspberry and banana muffins

Delicious warm or cold, for breakfast or tea, these muffins are also ideal for packed lunches and they freeze well. Another time, use blueberries instead of the raspberries to ring the changes.

150 g/10 tablespoons butter

2 very ripe bananas

150 ml/⅔ cup milk

150 g/¾ cup (caster) sugar

3 large eggs

300 g/2⅓ cups self-raising flour

1 slightly rounded teaspoon baking powder

150 g/1½ cups raspberries

3–4 tablespoons demerara sugar

2 tablespoons sunflower seeds

a 12-hole muffin pan, lined with muffin cases

Makes 12

Preheat the oven to 200°C (400°F) Gas 6.

Melt the butter in a small pan and let cool slightly.

Peel and mash the bananas.

In a large mixing bowl and using a balloon whisk, whisk together the milk, (caster) sugar, eggs and melted butter.

Sift in the flour and baking powder and add the raspberries and banana. Using a large metal spoon, fold everything together until combined, but don't over-mix.

Divide the mixture between the muffin cases. Sprinkle each muffin with a little demerara sugar and the sunflower seeds. Bake the muffins for 30–35 minutes, or until risen and golden. Let cool on a wire rack.

blueberry lime friands

If you haven't come across friands before, you will soon be converted. Based on the French *financier*, they are small, light-textured cakes. If you don't want to invest in a special friand pan, you can make these in a regular muffin pan.

125 g/1 stick butter

75 g/½ cup shelled, blanched hazelnuts

125 g/¾ cup icing/confectioners' sugar

100 g/¾ cup plain/all-purpose flour

finely grated zest of 2 limes

175 g/1⅓ cups blueberries

4 large egg whites

Lime syrup

freshly squeezed juice of 1 small lime

40 g/3 tablespoons (caster) sugar

a 9-hole friand pan, well buttered

Makes 9

Preheat the oven to 200°C (400°F) Gas 6.

Melt the butter in a small pan and let cool slightly.

Whiz the hazelnuts in a blender until finely ground.

Sift the icing/confectioners' sugar and flour into a large mixing bowl. Stir in the ground hazelnuts, lime zest and blueberries.

Put the egg whites in a large, scrupulously clean bowl and whisk until they form soft peaks. Using a large metal spoon, fold half the egg whites into the flour mixture with half the melted butter – be as gentle as you can be. Fold in the other half of the egg whites and melted butter.

Divide the mixture between the holes of the prepared friand pan. Bake in the preheated oven for 20 minutes.

To make the lime syrup, heat the lime juice and sugar together in a small pan, stirring, until all the sugar has dissolved.

Let the cooked friands cool for 5 minutes, then make a few holes in the top of each one using the point of a small, sharp knife. Carefully drizzle a little of the lime syrup over each of the warm cakes, allowing it to seep into the holes. Leave the friands in the pan until completely cold, before running a knife around the edges and turning them out.

vanilla cupcakes with raspberry frosting

These cakes, with their pretty pink frosting, are ideal for little girls' birthday parties and a good recipe to make with children. If you want to turn these into grown-up cakes, use the same frosting, but top each one with a fresh raspberry.

175 g/1½ sticks butter, softened and cubed

175 g/¾ cup (caster) sugar

3 large eggs

175 g/1⅓ cups self-raising flour, sifted

3 tablespoons milk

1 teaspoon vanilla extract

tiny sugar balls, sprinkles or pink edible glitter, to decorate

Raspberry frosting

75 g/5 tablespoons unsalted butter

60 g/⅖ cup raspberries

75 g/⅓ cup (caster) sugar

150 g/5 oz. cream cheese, chilled

a 12-hole muffin pan, lined with cupcake cases

Makes 10

Preheat the oven to 180°C (350°F) Gas 4.

Put the butter, sugar, eggs and flour in an electric mixer (or use a large mixing bowl and an electric whisk). Whisk together for a few minutes to combine. Add the milk and vanilla extract and whisk again.

Divide the mixture between the cupcake cases. Bake in the preheated oven for 25–30 minutes, or until risen and golden. Let cool on a wire rack.

To make the raspberry frosting, melt the butter in a small pan and let cool slightly.

Put the raspberries in a separate small pan and heat up – just until they reach simmering point and become a seedy purée. Take the pan off the heat and tip the purée into a coarse sieve/strainer set over a small bowl. Strain the purée, let the juice cool and discard the seeds.

Whisk together the sugar and cream cheese. Add the melted butter and whisk again. Finally, add 2 teaspoons of the cooled raspberry juice and mix again. You are aiming for a pretty pink colour, so add more juice as necessary. Chill the frosting until the cupcakes have completely cooled.

Top each cake with pink frosting – you can spread it on with a spatula, or use a piping bag, as you wish. Decorate with sugar balls, sprinkles or edible glitter.

ginger meringues

Meringues really are easy to make and, if you want to get ahead, they will keep for a couple of days in an airtight tin before sandwiching together.

3 large egg whites

185 g/1 scant cup (caster) sugar

1 ball stem ginger in syrup, drained and finely chopped

Ginger cream

150 ml/⅔ cup double/heavy cream

1 ball stem ginger in syrup, drained and finely chopped

2 baking sheets, lined with baking parchment (don't grease them, or your egg whites will collapse!)

Makes 15

Preheat the oven to 140°C (275°F) Gas 1.

Put the egg whites in a large, scrupulously clean bowl and whisk until they form stiff peaks. Now, gradually add the sugar – in tablespoonfuls – whisking all the time. You will end up with a smooth, thick, glossy meringue. Using a large metal spoon, gently fold in the chopped ginger.

Using a teaspoon, make 15 small mounds on each of the prepared baking sheets, swirling each mound into a peak using the end of a skewer. Each meringue should be about 4–5 cm/2 inches in diameter at the base.

Bake in the preheated oven for 30 minutes, then turn off the oven and leave the meringues in it until completely cold, ideally overnight.

To make the ginger cream, whip the cream until it forms soft peaks, then stir in the chopped ginger. Use to sandwich the meringues together in pairs.

mini chocolate, beet and cherry cakes

Using beet(root) in these gives them slightly soft, moist centres and they freeze well, before decorating. If they are a gift, dust them with cocoa, then sprinkle with edible mini gold balls – dip your finger in water before applying so that they stick.

75 g/2½ oz. dark/bittersweet chocolate (about 50% cocoa solids)

50 g/⅓ cup dried sour cherries or cranberries

175 g/1⅓ cups self-raising flour

40 g/⅓ cup cocoa powder

175 g/¾ cup light muscovado or packed light brown soft sugar

250 ml/1 cup groundnut or vegetable oil

3 large eggs

a pinch of salt

150 g/5 oz. cooked, peeled beet(root)

a 9-hole petite loaf pan (holes measuring 5.5 x 8 cm/ 2½ x 3⅜ in. and 2.5 cm/1½ in. deep), lined with mini-loaf cases

Makes 9

Preheat the oven to 180°C (350°F) Gas 4.

Break the chocolate into pieces and melt it in a heatproof bowl set over a pan of barely simmering water. Stir, then let cool slightly.

Roughly chop the sour cherries.

Sift the flour into an electric mixer (or use a large mixing bowl and an electric whisk). Add the cocoa, sugar, oil, eggs, salt and the melted chocolate, and whisk until combined. Using the coarse side of a grater, grate the beet(root) into the mixture and sprinkle in the chopped sour cherries. Using a large metal spoon, fold everything together gently.

Divide the mixture between the loaf cases. Bake in the preheated oven for 20–25 minutes, or until well risen. Let the cakes cool completely in the pan.

Note: The petite loaf pan and matching cases needed for these cakes can be bought from www.janeasher.co.uk and www.wilton.com. If you prefer, you can bake the cakes in muffin cases instead of mini-loaf cases – they will take 25–30 minutes in the oven, and make 9 muffins.

honey and rosemary madeleines

I like to use eucalyptus or Greek honey to make these, as it partners well with the delicate flavour of the rosemary, but you can, of course, use any honey. If you want to keep things really simple, they are equally delicious without the rosemary. Madeleines are best eaten fresh on the day of baking, but they do freeze well.

75 g/5 tablespoons butter

2 tablespoons (runny) honey

2 fresh rosemary sprigs

2 large eggs

100 g/½ cup (caster) sugar

50 g/⅓ cup self-raising flour

½ teaspoon baking powder

50 g/½ cup ground almonds

a small pinch of salt

a 12-hole madeleine pan, well buttered and lightly dusted with flour

Makes 18

Put the butter, honey and sprigs of rosemary in a small pan over the lowest possible heat. Heat gently, giving it a swirl now and then. Take the pan off the heat and let the mixture cool and infuse for 15 minutes.

Put the eggs and sugar in an electric mixer (or use a large mixing bowl and an electric whisk) and whisk until pale and mousse-like – this can take up to 10 minutes.

Preheat the oven to 200°C (400°F) Gas 6.

Sift the flour into a mixing bowl and stir in the baking powder, almonds and salt. Add half the melted butter mixture (removing the sprigs of rosemary as you do so) and half the flour mixture to the beaten eggs and sugar. Using a large metal spoon, fold everything together quickly but gently. Repeat this process with the remaining melted butter mixture and the flour mixture.

Fill the holes of the madeleine pan with mixture. Bake the madeleines in the preheated oven for 8–10 minutes, or until golden and risen. Let the madeleines cool in the pan for a couple of minutes, then remove (you may need a table knife to help ease them out) and transfer to a wire rack. Wash, re-grease and re-flour the pan before baking the remaining mixture. You will make about 18 madeleines in total depending on the size of the holes in your pan.

plum, orange and double almond crumble tartlets

If you are not a confident pastry maker, you shouldn't have any problems here, as this is a well-behaved pastry recipe. These tarts can also be turned into mince pies for Christmas – just substitute the jam and plums with 400 g/3 cups mincemeat.

Pastry base

200 g/1½ cups plain/all-purpose flour

100 g/6½ tablespoons unsalted butter, softened

1 tablespoon icing/confectioners' sugar, plus extra for dusting (optional)

1 large egg, lightly beaten

Crumble filling

75 g/⅓ cup demerara sugar

25 g/2 tablespoons unsalted butter, chilled and cubed

50 g/⅓ cup plain/all-purpose flour

3 tablespoons rolled oats

1 rounded tablespoon flaked/slivered almonds

grated zest of 1 large orange (use a zester, if you have one, rather than a fine grater)

3 ripe but firm plums

25 g/2 tablespoons shelled almonds (skin on)

7–8 tablespoons plum jam, such as Victoria or damson

a fluted 9-cm/3½-in. cookie cutter

2 x 12-hole muffin pans, oiled

Makes 24

To make the pastry base, put the flour, butter and icing/confectioners' sugar in an electric mixer. Mix for a minute or until the mixture resembles breadcrumbs. Add the egg and briefly mix again. As soon as the pastry starts to come together, tip it onto the work surface and bring it together in a ball. Press the ball into a disc, wrap in clingfilm/plastic wrap and chill it for 30 minutes.

To make the crumble filling, briefly mix the sugar, butter and flour in the electric mixer, again until the mixture resembles breadcrumbs. Stir in the oats, flaked/slivered almonds and orange zest.

On a lightly floured work surface, roll out the pastry until it is about 2 mm/⅛ inch thick. It may be easier to roll out half at a time. Using the cutter, stamp out rounds and use to line the holes of the pans – the pastry will come about halfway up the side of each hole. Gently re-form and re-roll the pastry, then keep stamping out rounds until you have 24. Chill the pastry-lined pans for 30 minutes.

Meanwhile, halve, pit and chop the plums into pea-sized pieces. Roughly chop the whole almonds.

Preheat the oven to 200°C (400°F) Gas 6.

Put a teaspoon of jam in each pastry case, then divide the chopped plum between them, followed by the crumble. Sprinkle each with chopped almonds.

Bake the tartlets in the preheated oven for 15–18 minutes, or until golden. Let cool for 5 minutes, then transfer to a wire rack. Eat warm or cold but not hot, as the jam will burn easily. Dust with icing/confectioners' sugar.

coffee and pecan cupcakes with praline

These are best made and eaten on the same day, but the undecorated cakes will keep well in the freezer if you want to make a batch to decorate later.

3 tablespoons instant coffee granules

6 tablespoons boiling water

275 g/1¼ cups (caster) sugar, plus 2 tablespoons

175 g/1⅛ sticks butter, softened and cubed

3 large eggs

175 g/1⅛ cups self-raising flour

100 g/⅞ cup pecans, chopped

Frosting

200 g/1 cup icing/confectioners' sugar

2 tablespoons crème fraîche

150 g/10 tablespoons unsalted butter, softened

2 x 12-hole muffin pans, lined with cupcake cases

a baking sheet, lined with baking parchment

Makes 15

Preheat the oven to 180°C (350°F) Gas 4.

Tip the coffee into a cup with the boiling water and the 2 tablespoons of (caster) sugar. Stir together for a minute or so until the sugar has dissolved. Let cool.

Put the butter, 175 g/¾ cup of the (caster) sugar and the eggs in the bowl of an electric mixer (or use a large mixing bowl and an electric whisk). Sift in the flour, drizzle in 3 tablespoons of the coffee syrup and whisk together for a few minutes to combine. Stir half the pecans into the mixture; reserve the other half for the praline.

Divide the mixture between the cupcake cases. Bake in the preheated oven for 20 minutes, or until risen and lightly golden. Transfer the cupcakes to a wire rack. While they are still warm, make a few fork indentations in the top of each one and carefully drizzle over a little of the remaining coffee syrup, letting it seep into the cakes as you do so. Let cool completely.

Next, make the praline. Tip the remaining 100 g/½ cup (caster) sugar into a medium pan or frying pan over low heat and heat gently. As soon as it has melted, increase the heat a little and let the sugar simmer and gradually turn to a deep golden caramel. Tip in the reserved pecans, give everything a quick stir and tip the hot praline onto the prepared baking sheet. Spread it out slightly, then leave until cold and set.

To make the frosting, sift the icing/confectioners' sugar into a bowl, add the crème fraîche and the butter and beat together until smooth.

Spread the frosting onto the cold cupcakes with a round-bladed knife. Bash the praline with the end of a rolling pin to break it up, then crumble some on top of each cake.

spiced pumpkin cheesecakes with nutmeg icing

Have fun with these for Halloween – use themed cupcake cases and decorate with sugarcraft sprinkles.

Cheesecakes

75 g/5 tablespoons butter

125 g/4 oz. shortcake or shortbread biscuits/graham crackers, broken into pieces

200 g/6½ oz. cream cheese

100 g/½ cup soft curd cheese or cottage cheese

100 g/½ cup canned pumpkin purée

100 g/½ cup (caster) sugar

2 medium eggs, lightly beaten

2 pinches each of ground cloves, ginger, allspice and nutmeg

orange sanding sugar, to decorate (optional)

Nutmeg icing

50 g/¼ cup (caster) sugar

100 g/3½ oz. cream cheese

½ teaspoon freshly grated nutmeg

a 12-hole muffin pan, lined with cupcake cases

Makes 12

Preheat the oven to 150°C (300°F) Gas 3.

First make the base for the cheesecakes. Melt the butter in a small pan and let cool slightly.

Grind the biscuits/crackers to crumbs in a food processor. Add all but 1 tablespoon of the melted butter (reserve this for the icing) and whiz to combine. Divide between the cupcake cases and press down with a teaspoon.

Put the cream cheese, curd cheese, pumpkin purée, sugar, beaten eggs and spices in an electric mixer (or use a large mixing bowl and an electric whisk). Whisk until smooth and combined. Tip the mixture into a jug, then pour it into the cupcake cases, dividing it equally.

Bake the cakes in the preheated oven for 15 minutes. Let cool completely – they will set as they cool.

To make the nutmeg icing, whisk the ingredients together (including the reserved butter) and put a spoonful on each cheesecake. If you are not eating them immediately, refrigerate them but let them come to room temperature before eating. Sprinkle with sanding sugar, if you like. They are soft-set, so they are best eaten with teaspoons.

cookies

prune, cinnamon and toasted walnut cookies with cinnamon icing

Agen prunes are a juicy and delicious addition to these chewy cookies, but raisins would also be a good choice. If you are making the cookies at Christmastime or are feeling decadent, substitute half the water in the icing with Armagnac.

75 g/½ cup walnut pieces

100 g/6½ tablespoons butter, softened

150 g/¾ cup packed light brown soft sugar

1 large egg, lightly beaten

2 tablespoons cream cheese

75 g/⅗ cup light brown/ whole-wheat and 75 g/⅗ cup white self-raising flour (or use all white flour)

2 teaspoons ground cinnamon

a pinch of salt

125 g/1 cup pitted, soft Agen prunes, snipped into small pieces

Cinnamon icing

50 g/¼ cup icing/ confectioners' sugar

2 or 3 pinches of ground cinnamon

2 baking sheets, oiled

Makes about 20

Preheat the oven to 200°C (400°F) Gas 6.

Spread the walnuts on a baking sheet and toast in the preheated oven for 5 minutes, then let cool.

Put the butter and sugar in an electric mixer (or use a large mixing bowl and an electric whisk) and beat until light and fluffy. Add the egg and cream cheese and mix again to combine. Sift in the flours (add any bran left in the sieve/strainer from the brown/whole-wheat flour, if using), the cinnamon and salt and mix again. Fold in the toasted walnuts and prunes with a large metal spoon.

Drop craggy mounds of the mixture onto the prepared baking sheets – about 1 rounded dessertspoonful each. Leave room between them to allow the cookies to spread as they bake; 6 or 7 per baking sheet is about right, so you will need to cook them in batches. Bake the cookies in the preheated oven for 10–12 minutes, or until golden. Let cool for a few minutes, then transfer to a wire rack to cool completely.

To make the cinnamon icing, sift the icing/confectioners' sugar and cinnamon into a small bowl. Add 2 teaspoons cold water and mix – you want a drizzling consistency, so add a few more drops of water if needed. Drizzle a little icing over each cookie and let set.

apricot, cherry and pine nut oat cookies

These are speedy and ideal to make with children, as the mixture won't come to any harm if it is rolled and prodded by little fingers. For a more grown-up variation, omit the cherries and add a level teaspoon of chopped fennel seeds with the oats.

50 g/⅓ cup ready-to-eat dried apricots

50 g/⅓ cup undyed glacé cherries

25 g/3 tablespoons pine nuts

100 g/6½ tablespoons butter, softened

50 g/¼ cup light muscovado or packed light brown soft sugar

50 g/½ cup plain/all-purpose flour

100 g/⅔ cup porridge oats

2 baking sheets, oiled

Makes about 18

Preheat the oven to 190°C (375°F) Gas 5.

Chop the apricots and cherries into small pieces and roughly chop the pine nuts.

Put the butter, sugar, flour and oats in an electric mixer (or use a large mixing bowl and an electric whisk) and beat until combined. Stir in the chopped apricots, cherries and pine nuts.

Bring the cookie dough together with your hands. Break off walnut-sized pieces and roll them into balls.

Arrange the balls of dough on the prepared baking sheets and press each one to flatten it slightly. Bake the cookies in the preheated oven for 15–18 minutes, or until lightly golden. Transfer the cookies to a wire rack to cool.

mini peanut butter and maple refrigerator cookies

These small, chunky cookies are very simple to make. Once made and chilled, the dough will keep for a couple of weeks in the fridge, so you can bake the cookies as and when you need them. The dough also freezes well – defrost, then slice and bake.

175 g/1½ sticks butter, softened and cubed

150 g/¾ cup crunchy peanut butter

2 tablespoons maple syrup

175 g/generous ¾ cup light muscovado or packed light brown soft sugar

300 g/2⅓ cups plain/all-purpose flour, sifted

1 teaspoon baking powder

a pinch of salt

1 large egg, lightly beaten

demerara sugar, for sprinkling

2–3 baking sheets, oiled

Makes about 48

Put the butter, peanut butter, maple syrup and muscovado sugar in an electric mixer (or use a large mixing bowl and an electric whisk) and beat until combined. Tip in the flour, baking powder and salt and add the beaten egg. Beat to combine, then bring the dough together with your hands.

Tip the dough out onto a lightly floured surface and divide it into 4. Roll each quarter into a sausage shape about 16 cm/6½ inches in length and 3 cm/1¼ inches in diameter. Wrap each one in clingfilm/plastic wrap and refrigerate for 30 minutes. After that, when the cookie dough is firm, you can cut slices from it to bake as you wish.

To bake the cookies, preheat the oven to 200°C (400°F) Gas 6.

Slice 1½-cm/½-inch-thick circles of dough from the rolls; you should get about 12 cookies from each one.

Arrange the cookies on the prepared baking sheets. Lightly press the back of a fork into the top of each cookie to make an indentation and sprinkle with demerara sugar. Bake in the preheated oven for 10–12 minutes, or until golden. Let cool on wire racks.

salted caramel malt cookies

If you don't have a cutter the right size to make these, cut around a glass, the lid of a small pot or similar. They are also cute made as mini-cookies using a 3-cm/1¼-inch cutter. The sea salt adds a special something to the caramel, making the cookies dangerously good.

200 g/1⅔ cups self-raising flour

75 g/½ cup malted milk powder, e.g. Horlicks

a tiny pinch of salt

150 g/10 tablespoons butter, softened and cubed

50 g/¼ cup (caster) sugar

1 medium egg, lightly beaten

Salted caramel

75 g/⅓ cup dark muscovado or packed dark brown soft sugar

50 g/3 tablespoons butter

¼ teaspoon crushed sea salt, e.g. fleur de sel or Maldon

½ x 397-g/14-oz. can condensed milk

a plain 5-cm/2-in. cookie cutter

2 baking sheets, oiled

Makes about 24

Sift the flour into the bowl of an electric mixer. Add the malted milk powder, salt and butter. Mix together until the mixture resembles breadcrumbs.

Tip in the sugar and the beaten egg. Mix until combined, then bring the dough together with your hands. Wrap in clingfilm/plastic wrap and refrigerate for 30 minutes.

Preheat the oven to 190°C (375°F) Gas 5.

Tip half the dough out onto a lightly floured work surface and roll out until it is 8–9 mm/⅜ inch thick. Using the cutter, stamp out rounds, then gently re-form the dough and continue until you have used it all.

Arrange the cookies on the prepared baking sheets. Bake in the preheated oven for 10 minutes, or until golden. Let cool on wire racks.

Repeat with the other half of the dough.

To make the salted caramel, gently heat the sugar, butter and sea salt in a pan until the sugar has dissolved, stirring now and then. Tip in the condensed milk and heat over low heat for 5–6 minutes, stirring all the time, until the mixture is amalgamated. Increase the heat, and as soon as the caramel starts to bubble, take the pan off the heat. Let cool until barely warm.

Top each cookie with a swirl of the caramel, then let cool completely and set.

giant double chocolate chip cookies

Chewy and soft, these are a favourite to eat while still warm. I like chopping my own chocolate rather than using chocolate chips and often add a handful of roughly chopped unsalted shelled peanuts or hazelnuts too.

225 g/2 sticks butter, softened

100 g/½ cup light muscovado or packed light brown soft sugar

150 g/¾ cup demerara sugar

2 large eggs, lightly beaten

300 g/2¼ cups self-raising flour, sifted

½ teaspoon baking powder

a pinch of salt

125 g/4 oz. dark/bittersweet chocolate (about 50% cocoa solids)

125 g/4 oz. milk chocolate

2 baking sheets, lined with baking parchment

Makes about 16

Preheat the oven to 180°C (350°F) Gas 4.

Put the butter and sugars in an electric mixer (or use a large mixing bowl and an electric whisk) and beat for 3–4 minutes, or until creamy and fluffy. Add the beaten eggs and mix again.

Tip in the flour, baking powder and salt and mix. Chop both types of chocolate into small chunks, then, using a large metal spoon, stir the chunks into the mixture. Break off golf ball-sized pieces and roll them into balls.

Arrange the balls of dough on the prepared baking sheets. Leave room between them to allow the cookies to spread as they bake – they will end up being about 11–12 cm/4½ inches in diameter once cooked. You will need to cook them in batches. Bake in the preheated oven for 10–12 minutes, or until golden at the edges. Let cool for a couple of minutes, then transfer to a wire rack.

st. clement's macarons

Macarons have made a comeback in recent years and are now sold in all sorts of pretty colours. This is a simple way of making them and you can buy very good, luxury lemon or orange curd, which is ideal for filling them.

100 g/1 cup ground almonds

150 g/¾ cup (caster) sugar

2 teaspoons plain/
all-purpose flour

2 large egg whites

grated zest of 1 unwaxed lemon

grated zest of ½ orange

Filling

3 tablespoons cream cheese

3 tablespoons thick lemon or orange curd

grated zest of ½ orange

2 baking sheets, lined with baking parchment

Makes 12

Preheat the oven to 180°C (350°F) Gas 4.

Tip all the ingredients (other than those for the filling) into an electric mixer. Alternatively, put them in a large mixing bowl and use an electric whisk. Beat together until well combined.

Put 24 teaspoonfuls of the mixture onto the prepared baking sheets, leaving room for them to spread slightly. Bake in the preheated oven for 15–17 minutes, or until set and tinged with gold at the edges. Let cool for a few minutes, then transfer to wire racks.

To make the filling, whisk the cream cheese and curd together until smooth. Stir in the orange zest and refrigerate until needed. Sandwich the macarons together with the filling.

dark chocolate thins with white chocolate filling

These delicate but very chocolatey cookies have a thin layer of sweet filling. If you want to cheat, fill them with hazelnut chocolate spread instead.

125 g/1 stick butter, softened

50 g/¼ cup (caster) sugar

150 g/1 generous cup plain/all-purpose flour, sifted

2 tablespoons cocoa powder, plus extra for dusting

75 g/2½ oz. dark/bittersweet chocolate (about 50% cocoa solids), broken into pieces

1 tablespoon vegetable oil

White chocolate filling

75 g/2½ oz. white chocolate, broken into pieces

2 teaspoons (runny) honey

2 tablespoons crème fraîche

2 baking sheets, lined with baking parchment

Makes 10

Put the butter and sugar in an electric mixer (or use a large mixing bowl and an electric whisk) and beat until light and fluffy. Tip in the flour and cocoa and mix to combine. If the mixture doesn't come together instantly, work it briefly with a spatula, then mix again until it comes together in a ball. Wrap in clingfilm/plastic wrap and refrigerate for 30 minutes.

To make the white chocolate filling, put the chocolate pieces, honey and crème fraîche in a small heatproof bowl set over a pan of barely simmering water. Stir until the chocolate has melted and the mixture is smooth. Take the bowl off the heat, let cool, then refrigerate.

Preheat the oven to 160°C (325°F) Gas 3.

Lightly dust a work surface with cocoa. Halve the chilled dough and roll one half out on the work surface until it is about 5 mm/¼ inch thick. Cut out 10 rectangles, 7 x 4 cm/3 x 1½ inches, re-rolling the dough as necessary. Arrange the cookies on one baking sheet. Repeat with the other half of the dough.

Bake in the preheated oven for 10 minutes. Let cool for a few minutes, then transfer to wire racks.

Melt the dark/bittersweet chocolate with the oil as you did for the white chocolate above. Take the bowl off the heat and dip the opposite corners of half the cookies into it. Let set.

Bring the filling back to room temperature and give it a stir. Spread a layer of filling on the underside of each of the plain cookies and place a chocolate-dipped cookie on top.

passion-fruit sandwich cookies

These are dainty, melt-in-the-mouth cookies sandwiched together with a passion-fruit cream. Choose passion fruit that have wrinkled skins, as they will be the most fragrant and juicy.

500 g/4 sticks butter, softened

100 g/⅔ cup icing/confectioners' sugar, sifted, plus extra for dusting

400 g/3⅓ cups plain/all-purpose flour, sifted

100 g/¾ cup cornflour/cornstarch, sifted

Passion-fruit cream

100 g/5 tablespoons mascarpone

75 g/½ cup icing/confectioners' sugar, sifted

pulp of 2 passion fruit

a piping bag, fitted with a wide plain or star nozzle/tip

3 baking sheets, lined with baking parchment

Makes 14

Preheat the oven to 180°C (350°F) Gas 4.

Put the butter and sugar in an electric mixer (or use a large mixing bowl and an electric whisk) and beat together until pale and creamy. Tip in the flour and cornflour/cornstarch and whisk again to combine.

Fill the piping bag with the mixture and use to pipe 9-cm/3½-inch lengths onto the prepared baking sheets. Leave room between them to allow the cookies to spread as they bake. Bake in the preheated oven for 15–18 minutes, or until lightly golden at the edges. Let cool on the baking sheets.

To make the passion-fruit cream, mix all the ingredients together and refrigerate until needed.

Sandwich the cookies together with the passion-fruit cream. Lightly dust the top of each one with icing/confectioners' sugar.

bright-as-a-button cookies

These are fun to make and children will enjoy the brightly coloured icings. Experiment with different food colours or you can, of course, ice them all one colour. Alternatively, leave them plain, if you prefer.

Put the butter and sugar in an electric mixer (or use a large mixing bowl and an electric whisk) and beat together until pale and fluffy. Add the beaten egg, flour, ground almonds, baking powder and lemon juice and mix to combine.

Tip the dough onto a lightly floured work surface and bring it together in a ball. Press the ball into a disc, wrap in clingfilm/plastic wrap and refrigerate for at least 30 minutes.

Preheat the oven to 200°C (400°F) Gas 6.

Halve the chilled dough and roll one half out on the lightly floured work surface until it is about 5 mm/¼ inch thick. Cut out 5 x 10-cm/4-inch circles, using an upturned tea cup or similar to cut around. Arrange the cookies on one of the prepared baking sheets. Using the 1½-cm/½-inch cookie

cutter (or the tip of a small sharp knife), stamp out 2 rounds from the middle of each cookie to make buttonholes.

Repeat with the other half of the dough. Bake in the preheated oven for 10 minutes. Transfer to wire racks to cool.

To decorate, sift the icing/confectioners' sugar into a bowl and stir in 3–4 tablespoons cold water – add it little by little until you have a thick icing consistency; you may not need it all. Divide the icing between 3 bowls and add a touch of food colouring to each. Add it with the very tip of a small knife – you really don't need much. Mix thoroughly.

Spread icing on each of the buttons. Let set for about 30 minutes before threading ribbon through the buttonholes.

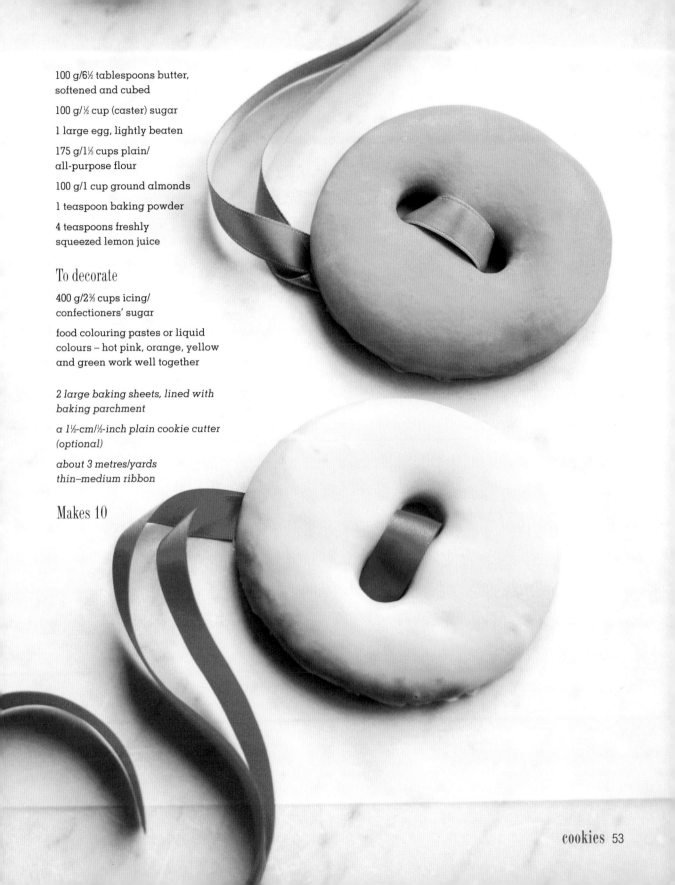

100 g/6½ tablespoons butter, softened and cubed

100 g/½ cup (caster) sugar

1 large egg, lightly beaten

175 g/1⅓ cups plain/ all-purpose flour

100 g/1 cup ground almonds

1 teaspoon baking powder

4 teaspoons freshly squeezed lemon juice

To decorate

400 g/2⅔ cups icing/ confectioners' sugar

food colouring pastes or liquid colours – hot pink, orange, yellow and green work well together

2 large baking sheets, lined with baking parchment

a 1½-cm/½-inch plain cookie cutter (optional)

about 3 metres/yards thin–medium ribbon

Makes 10

spiced brown sugar and clementine stars

These crisp, spiced cookies are pretty baked as stars but you can experiment with other shapes – hearts are cute too. If you are making them to hang on a Christmas tree, as soon as they come out of the oven make holes at one end of each cookie using a skewer, to thread ribbon through later.

100 g/6½ tablespoons butter, softened and cubed

75 g/⅓ cup dark muscovado or packed dark brown soft sugar

1 teaspoon golden/corn syrup

1 medium egg, lightly beaten

200 g/1⅔ cups plain/all-purpose flour, sifted

1 teaspoon baking powder

grated zest of 1 clementine

2 teaspoons ground cinnamon

a generous pinch each of ground nutmeg, allspice and cloves

To decorate

100 g/⅔ cup icing/confectioners' sugar

6–7 teaspoons freshly squeezed lemon juice

edible silver balls

edible white glitter

star cookie cutters in various sizes

2 large baking sheets, lined with baking parchment

Makes about 30

Put the butter, sugar and golden/corn syrup in an electric mixer (or use a large mixing bowl and an electric whisk) and mix until combined. Add the beaten egg little by little, alternating with a spoonful of flour, and still mixing. Add the rest of the flour, the baking powder, clementine zest and spices. Mix to combine.

Tip the dough onto a lightly floured work surface and bring it together in a ball. Press the ball into a disc, wrap in clingfilm/plastic wrap and refrigerate for at least 30 minutes.

Preheat the oven to 200°C (400°F) Gas 6.

Halve the chilled dough and roll one half out on the lightly floured work surface until it is about 5 mm/³⁄₁₆ inch thick. Cut out stars with the cookie cutters and arrange the cookies on one of the prepared baking sheets. Gently re-form and re-roll the dough, then keep stamping out stars.

Repeat with the other half of the dough. Bake in the preheated oven for 8–10 minutes for smaller stars (about 6 cm/2½ inches) and 12–14 minutes for larger stars (about 8.5 cm/3½ inches). When they are ready, the dough will have risen slightly and the edges will be tinged with brown. Transfer to wire racks to cool.

To decorate, sift the icing/confectioners' sugar into a bowl and stir in the lemon juice – add it little by little until you have a drizzling consistency. Decorate each star with a little icing (you can pipe it if you are feeling fancy). Finish with edible silver balls and glitter.

gingerbread men

The gingerbread men are crisp when baked, so are pretty resilient for children to ice them with tubes of ready-made icing, if that should appeal.

100 g/6½ tablespoons butter

50 g/¼ cup dark muscovado or packed dark brown soft sugar

225 g/1¾ cups plain/all-purpose flour

¾ teaspoon bicarbonate of/baking soda

2 teaspoons ground ginger

1 teaspoon ground cinnamon

4 tablespoons golden/corn syrup

1 tablespoon black treacle/blackstrap molasses

small coloured sugar-coated chocolate drops or halved currants, for decoration

a 7–8-cm/3-inch (top to bottom) gingerbread man cutter

2 baking sheets, lightly buttered

Makes about 18

Heat the butter and sugar together in a small pan until melted, stirring every now and then. Remove the pan from the heat and let cool slightly.

Sift the flour, bicarbonate of/baking soda, and ground ginger and cinnamon into the bowl of an electric mixer (or use a large mixing bowl and an electric whisk) and pour the melted butter mixture into it. Add the golden/corn syrup and treacle/molasses and mix to combine. Bring together into a ball, wrap in clingfilm/plastic wrap and refrigerate for 30 minutes.

Preheat the oven to 190°C (375°F) Gas 5.

Halve the chilled dough and roll one half out on the lightly floured work surface until it is about 5–6 mm/¼ inch thick. Cut out men with the cutter and arrange them on one of the prepared baking sheets. Gently re-form and re-roll the dough, then keep stamping out gingerbread men. Make indentations for eyes and mouths and add sugar-coated chocolate drops or currants for buttons.

Repeat with the other half of the dough.

Bake the gingerbread men in the preheated oven for 8 minutes, or until they are set and slightly firmer to the touch. Transfer to wire racks to cool.

brownies
& bars

hazelnut cheesecake bars

These bars will keep in the fridge for a day or so. They are ideal for coffee time or they also double up well as a simple pudding with poached fruit alongside.

200 g/1½ cups shelled, blanched hazelnuts

75 g/5 tablespoons butter

200 g/6½ oz. ginger nut biscuits/gingersnaps, broken into pieces

icing/confectioners' sugar, for dusting

Cheesecake topping

400 g/14 oz. cream cheese

175 g/¾ cup (caster) sugar

3 large eggs

300 ml/1¼ cups sour cream

a 20 x 33 x 3–4-cm/9 x 13-in. baking pan, oiled

Makes 14

Preheat the oven to 180°C (350°F) Gas 4.

Spread the hazelnuts on a baking sheet and toast in the preheated oven for 10–12 minutes, then let cool. Reduce the oven temperature to 160°C (325°F) Gas 3.

Melt the butter in a small pan and let cool slightly.

Tip the biscuits/gingersnaps into a food processor. Add half the cooled hazelnuts and whiz together until you have fine crumbs. Add the melted butter and briefly whiz again. Tip the mixture into the prepared baking pan and press down firmly with the back of a spoon to make an even layer. Put the pan on a baking sheet.

To make the cheesecake topping, put all the ingredients in an electric mixer (or use a large mixing bowl and an electric whisk) and whisk to combine. Carefully pour the mixture on top of the crust in the pan – the mixture will come pretty near the top. Roughly chop the remaining hazelnuts and scatter over the cheesecake. Bake in the preheated oven for 45 minutes. Let cool completely.

Refrigerate for 30 minutes before cutting into 14 bars with a sharp knife. The cheesecake will be soft-set. Lightly dust with icing/confectioners' sugar.

chocolate fudge raspberry shortbread bars

This is a sophisticated, bite-size number; the tart fruitiness of the raspberries complements the dark/bittersweet chocolate.

125 g/1 stick butter, softened

50 g/¼ cup granulated sugar

150 g/1 generous cup plain/all-purpose flour

Chocolate topping

400 ml/1¾ cups double/heavy cream

2 tablespoons icing/confectioners' sugar

400 g/14 oz. dark/bittersweet chocolate (70% cocoa solids), chopped

200 g/1½ cups raspberries

a 20-cm/8-in. square pan, ideally loose-based, oiled

Makes 21

Preheat the oven to 190°C (375°F) Gas 5.

Put the butter and sugar in an electric mixer and beat for 3–4 minutes, or until pale and creamy. Tip in the flour and mix again for a few minutes to combine – the dough probably won't come together in a ball, but if you work it briefly with a wooden spoon and then your hands, it will come together. Tip into the prepared pan and press down firmly with the back of a spoon to make an even layer. Prick the base a few times with a fork. Bake in the preheated oven for 20 minutes, or until lightly golden. Let cool.

To make the chocolate topping, bring the cream and icing/confectioners' sugar slowly to the boil in a pan. Put the chocolate in a heatproof bowl. As soon as the cream begins to bubble, remove from the heat and pour into the bowl with the chocolate. Gently whisk together until the chocolate has melted and the mixture is smooth.

Stir the raspberries into the chocolate mixture, then pour it over the cooled crust in the square pan. Let cool completely, then refrigerate for 3 hours, or until set. Cut into 21 bars with a sharp knife.

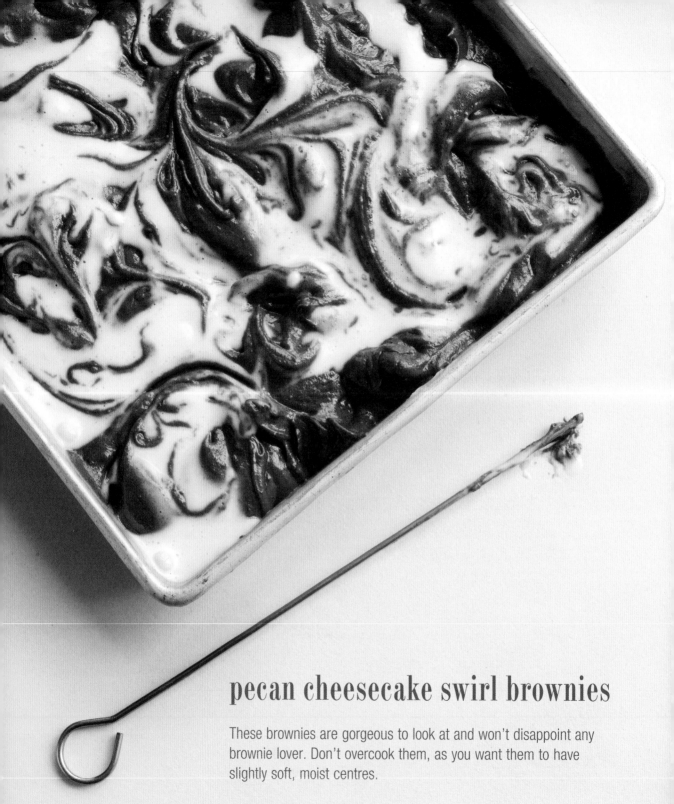

pecan cheesecake swirl brownies

These brownies are gorgeous to look at and won't disappoint any brownie lover. Don't overcook them, as you want them to have slightly soft, moist centres.

100 g/⅞ cup pecan halves

100 g/3½ oz. dark/bittersweet chocolate (70% cocoa solids), broken into pieces

100 g/6½ tablespoons butter, softened

200 g/1 cup light muscovado or packed light brown soft sugar

2 large eggs, lightly beaten

100 g/¾ cup plain/all-purpose flour, sifted

Cheesecake swirl

1 large egg

150 g/5 oz. cream cheese

3 tablespoons sugar

1 tablespoon plain/all-purpose flour

an 18-cm/7-in. square pan, oiled and baselined with baking parchment

Makes 16

Preheat the oven to 180°C (350°F) Gas 4.

Spread the pecans on a baking sheet and toast in the preheated oven for 10 minutes, then let cool.

Melt the chocolate pieces in a small heatproof bowl set over a pan of barely simmering water. Remove the bowl from the heat and let cool a little.

Roughly chop the toasted pecans.

Put the butter and sugar in an electric mixer (or use a large mixing bowl and an electric whisk) and beat until combined. Gradually add the beaten eggs, still mixing. Tip in the flour and add the slightly cooled melted chocolate. Mix again until combined. Using a large metal spoon, fold in the chopped pecans.

To make the cheesecake swirl, whisk all the ingredients together in a bowl until combined.

Tip the chocolate mixture into the prepared pan and spread it evenly with a spatula. Drop blobs of the cheesecake mixture on top and, using a skewer or the end of a teaspoon, briefly swirl the cheesecake mixture into the top of the chocolate layer.

Bake the brownies in the preheated oven for 25 minutes. Let cool completely before cutting into 16 squares.

spiced date, apple and sticky oat slices

My mother used to make these for me when I was revising for school exams, so we called them exam slices. I still love them.

250 g/1½ cups pitted, soft dates, chopped

2 tart dessert apples, cored, peeled and chopped

finely grated zest of 1 orange

freshly squeezed juice of 2 oranges

1 teaspoon freshly squeezed lemon juice

1 teaspoon mixed/apple pie spice

Sticky oat layer

100 g/⅔ cup porridge oats

100 g/½ cup (caster) sugar

100 g/¾ cup self-raising flour

50 g/3 tablespoons butter, softened and cubed

50 g/3 tablespoons golden/corn syrup

1 large egg yolk

an 18-cm/7-in. square pan, ideally loose-based, oiled

Makes 10

Tip the chopped dates, apples, orange zest and juice, lemon juice and spice into a medium pan. Mix and heat over medium heat. Once everything has come to simmering point, reduce the heat to low and gently cook the fruit for 8–10 minutes, covered, until the apple has softened. Let cool.

Preheat the oven to 180°C (350°F) Gas 4.

To make the sticky oat layer, put all the ingredients in an electric mixer (or use a large mixing bowl and an electric whisk) and beat to combine. Tip half this mixture into the base of the prepared pan and press down firmly with the back of a spoon to make an even layer.

Spoon the cooled date and apple mixture on top of the sticky oat base and top with the remaining sticky oat layer, pressing it down again to make an even layer. Bake in the preheated oven for 30 minutes. Let cool completely before cutting into 10 bars.

coconut, apricot and lime slices

These are a modern version of the coconut slice. The traditional version has raspberry jam beneath the coconut topping, but I think these are all the better for their juicy apricot layer.

125 g/1 stick butter, softened

50 g/¼ cup demerara sugar

150 g/1 generous cup plain/all-purpose flour

450 g/1 lb. ready-to-eat dried apricots, finely chopped

grated zest and freshly squeezed juice of 3 limes

Coconut topping

2 large eggs

1 x 160-ml/5½-oz. can coconut cream

50 g/¼ cup (caster) sugar

125 g/1 scant cup desiccated coconut

a 20 x 33 x 3–4-cm/9 x 13-in. baking pan, oiled

Makes 14

Preheat the oven to 180°C (350°F) Gas 4.

Put the butter and sugar in an electric mixer and beat for 3–4 minutes, or until pale and creamy. Tip in the flour and mix again for a few minutes to combine.

Tip the mixture into the prepared pan and press down firmly with the back of a spoon to make an even layer. Prick the base a few times with a fork. Bake in the preheated oven for 15–20 minutes, or until lightly golden. Leave the oven on.

Meanwhile, put the apricots and lime zest and juice in a medium pan with 4 tablespoons cold water and bring to simmering point. Gently cook, covered, for 8–10 minutes, or until soft and mushy. Add another tablespoon of water if the mixture seems too dry as it simmers. Let the apricots cool slightly, then transfer to a food processor and whiz to a thick purée.

To make the coconut topping, lightly beat the eggs in the electric mixer, then add the coconut cream, sugar and desiccated coconut and mix to combine.

Spread the apricot purée on top of the baked base and top with the coconut mixture, spreading it evenly. Bake for 40–45 minutes, or until golden. Let cool completely before cutting into 14 slices.

cherry marzipan streusel squares

These are also a favourite when made with raspberry or plum jam.

100 g/¾ cup plain/
all-purpose flour

50 g/3 tablespoons butter,
chilled and diced

1 tablespoon icing/
confectioners' sugar

5 tablespoons morello
cherry jam

Streusel topping

75 g/⅖ cup plain/all-purpose
flour

75 g/⅓ cup granulated sugar

25 g/2 tablespoons butter,
softened and cubed

50 g/1¾ oz. marzipan, diced

50 g/⅕ cup undyed glacé/
candied cherries, chopped

50 g/½ cup flaked/slivered
almonds

Almond layer

100 g/6½ tablespoons butter,
softened and cubed

75 g/⅛ cup (caster) sugar

2 large eggs, lightly beaten

100 g/1 cup ground almonds

3 tablespoons plain/
all-purpose flour

*an 18-cm/7-in. square pan,
ideally loose-based, oiled*

Makes 12

For the pastry, put the flour, butter and sugar in an electric mixer and whiz until the mixture resembles breadcrumbs. Add 2 tablespoons cold water and whiz again. Add a few more drops of water, if needed, to bring together into a dough.

Tip the pastry out on a lightly floured work surface and roll out until it is about 3–4 mm/⅛ inch thick. Trim the edges with a sharp knife to make a 19-cm/7½-inch square. Line the base of the pan with the pastry – it will come slightly up the inside of the pan all the way round. Refrigerate for 30 minutes.

Preheat the oven to 200°C (400°F) Gas 6.

To make the streusel topping, tip the flour and sugar into the electric mixer (or use a mixing bowl and an electric whisk) and whiz together. Add the butter and whiz until the mixture is crumbly. Tip into a bowl, if necessary, and stir in the marzipan, glacé/candied cherries and flaked/slivered almonds.

To make the almond layer, mix all the ingredients together in the electric mixer until amalgamated.

Spread the cherry jam on top of the chilled pastry base. Spoon blobs of the almond mixture on top of the jam and spread them out with a spatula. Scatter the streusel topping over the top. Put the pan on a baking sheet and bake in the preheated oven for 40 minutes, or until lightly golden. Cover with foil towards the end of cooking to prevent over-browning. Let cool in the pan before cutting into 12 squares.

throw-together muesli bars

These are a really quick assembly job and will keep in an airtight container for several days, and they freeze well too. Perfect for picnics, long walks and lunchboxes.

100 g/6½ tablespoons butter

4 tablespoons golden/corn syrup

75 g/⅓ cup (caster) sugar

225 g/1¾ cups jumbo rolled oats

125 g/1 cup ready-to-eat dried apricots, chopped

100 g/¾ cup pitted, soft dates, chopped

4 tablespoons sultanas/golden raisins

4 tablespoons chopped pistachios

3 tablespoons chopped brazil nuts

3 tablespoons sesame seeds

1 tablespoon freshly squeezed lemon juice

a 20-cm/8-in. square pan, ideally loose-based, well oiled

Makes 8

Preheat the oven to 190°C (375°F) Gas 5.

Heat the butter and golden/corn syrup together in a small pan until melted.

Meanwhile, combine all the other ingredients in a large mixing bowl. Add the warm butter mixture and stir thoroughly to combine.

Tip the mixture into the prepared pan and press down firmly with the back of a spoon to make an even layer. Bake in the preheated oven for 25 minutes, or until golden. Let cool for 15 minutes or so, then, using a sharp knife, carefully cut into 8 bars. Let cool completely before lifting the bars out of the pan.

nectarine and blueberry bars with lavender sugar

These bars are packed full of juicy fruit. You can leave out the lavender if it isn't your thing and the nectarines can be swapped for peaches, a similar quantity of plums or apricots, or 250 g/1 pint of mixed berries. In any case, the bars are best made and eaten on the same day.

3 large eggs

200 g/1 cup (caster) sugar

175 g/1¼ cups self-raising flour, sifted

1 teaspoon baking powder

½ teaspoon vanilla extract

175 g/1½ sticks butter, softened and cubed

½ tablespoon dried lavender buds

3 ripe but firm nectarines

200 g/1½ cups blueberries

1 tablespoon polenta (cornmeal)

Lavender sugar

½ tablespoon dried lavender buds

2 tablespoons (caster) sugar

grated zest of 1 unwaxed lemon

a 20 x 33 x 3–4-cm/9 x 13-in. baking pan, lined with baking parchment and lightly buttered

Serves 14

Preheat the oven to 180°C (350°F) Gas 4.

Put the eggs, sugar, flour, baking powder, vanilla extract, butter and lavender in an electric mixer (or use a large mixing bowl and an electric whisk) and whisk together. Pit the nectarines, chop them into bite-size pieces and stir into the mixture along with the blueberries.

Dust the bottom of the prepared pan with the polenta (cornmeal) and a very small amount of flour. Spoon the mixture into the pan and spread it evenly with a spatula.

To make the lavender sugar, mix the ingredients together in a bowl, then scatter evenly over the batter.

Bake in the preheated oven for 35 minutes, or until risen and golden. Let cool in the pan before cutting into 14 rectangles.

sticky toffee bars with toffee fudge drizzle

Another day, try replacing the ginger with 50 g/⅓ cup sultanas/golden raisins in the mix and use golden syrup or maple syrup in the icing instead of the ginger syrup.

175 g/1½ sticks butter, softened

125 g/½ cup dark muscovado or packed dark brown soft sugar

150 g/⅔ cup golden/corn syrup

75 g/¼ cup black treacle/blackstrap molasses

200 g/1½ cups self-raising flour

1 teaspoon vanilla extract

3 large eggs

2 tablespoons double/heavy cream

2 balls stem ginger in syrup, drained and finely chopped

Toffee fudge icing

50 g/3 tablespoons butter

1 tablespoon of the syrup from the jar of stem ginger

2 tablespoons double/heavy cream

75 g/⅓ cup dark muscovado or packed dark brown soft sugar

40 g/⅓ cup icing/confectioners' sugar

a 20 x 33 x 3–4-cm/9 x 13-in. baking pan, lined with baking parchment and lightly buttered

Serves 14

Preheat the oven to 180°C (350°F) Gas 4.

Put the butter, sugar, golden/corn syrup, treacle/molasses, flour, vanilla extract, eggs and cream in an electric mixer (or use a large mixing bowl and an electric whisk) and beat until combined. Stir in the stem ginger.

Tip the mixture into the prepared pan and spread it evenly with a spatula. Bake in the preheated oven for 25–30 minutes, or until risen and just set in the middle. Let cool completely in the pan.

To make the toffee fudge icing, put the butter, ginger syrup, cream and muscovado sugar in a medium pan over low heat and leave until the butter has melted and the sugar dissolved. Remove the pan from the heat, sift in the icing/confectioners' sugar, then whisk it in.

Remove the cake from the pan and drizzle the icing over it. Let set before cutting into 14 bars.

lemon squares

These look pretty as they are, lightly dusted with icing/confectioners' sugar, but I sometimes top each square with a slice of fig or strawberry too.

100 g/¾ cup plain/
all-purpose flour

35 g/¼ cup icing/
confectioners' sugar,
plus extra for dusting

75 g/5 tablespoons unsalted
butter, chilled and cubed

1–2 figs, very thinly sliced,
to decorate (optional)

Lemon layer

3 large eggs

275 g/1⅓ cups (caster) sugar

finely grated zest of
1 unwaxed lemon

150 ml/⅔ cup freshly
squeezed lemon juice
(from 3–4 lemons)

50 g/⅓ cup plain/all-purpose
flour, sifted

*an 18-cm/7-in. square pan,
oiled*

Makes 16

Preheat the oven to 180°C (350°F) Gas 4.

First prepare the pan. Place 2 wide strips of baking parchment from one side to the other of the pan so that they form a cross on the base – this will help you to lift the cake out of the pan when it is cooked. Place a square of baking parchment on top of the strips, as you would usually do to line the base of a pan.

Put the flour, icing/confectioners' sugar and butter in an electric mixer (or use a large mixing bowl and an electric whisk) and whiz until the mixture resembles breadcrumbs. Tip the mixture into the prepared pan and press down firmly with the back of a spoon to make an even layer. Prick the base a few times with a fork. Bake in the preheated oven for 12–15 minutes, or until lightly golden. Reduce the oven temperature to 150°C (300°F) Gas 3.

To make the lemon layer, put the eggs, sugar and lemon zest in the electric mixer and beat for a minute or so. With the beaters still going, gradually pour in the lemon juice, then tip in the flour and mix to combine.

Tip the mixture on top of the baked base. Bake for 45 minutes, by which time the lemon layer will be set and the top slightly crusty. Let cool completely.

Run a sharp knife around the edges, then lift out of the pan. Lightly dust with icing/confectioners' sugar and cut into 16 squares. Decorate with the slices of fig, if using.

in a flash

lime drizzle cake with coconut frosting

If you want to make this look extra special, add a few shavings of toasted fresh coconut to the top.

175 g/1½ sticks butter, softened

175 g/¾ cup (caster) sugar

175 g/1⅓ cups self-raising flour, sifted

3 eggs

finely grated zest of 2 limes

Lime drizzle

75 g/½ cup icing/confectioners' sugar

freshly squeezed juice of 2 limes

Coconut frosting

175 g/6 oz. cream cheese

5 tablespoons coconut cream

2 tablespoons icing/confectioners' sugar

grated zest of 1 lime (use a zester, if you have one, rather than a fine grater)

an 18-cm/7-in. round pan, 7 cm/3 in. deep, lightly buttered and baselined with baking parchment

Serves 8

Preheat the oven to 180°C (350°F) Gas 4.

Put the butter, sugar, flour, eggs and lime zest in an electric mixer (or use a large mixing bowl and an electric whisk) and beat until combined.

Spoon the mixture into the prepared pan and spread it evenly with a spatula. Bake in the preheated oven for 50–55 minutes, or until a skewer comes out clean when inserted into the centre of the cake.

Meanwhile, to make the lime drizzle, sift the icing/confectioners' sugar into a bowl and stir in the lime juice, then set aside.

To make the coconut frosting, whisk the cream cheese, coconut cream and icing/confectioners' sugar together in a bowl, then refrigerate until needed.

When the cake is ready, remove it from the oven and, using a small, fine skewer, make a few holes over the surface of the cake. Spoon over the lime drizzle (put the pan on a plate first if it is loose-based). Let the cake cool completely in its pan.

Once cold, pop the cake out of the pan, remove the base paper and spread the frosting over the top. Sprinkle with the lime zest.

simple fruit cake

This energy-giving cut-and-come-again cake is full of fruit and nuts and uses agave nectar – a low-GI, natural fructose sweetener – so a slice will keep hunger at bay. Agave nectar is now available in many supermarkets. If you want to make this cake more celebratory, brush warm, smooth apricot jam over it and decorate with small dried apricots and pecan halves.

100 g/⅔ cup ready-to-eat dried apricots or figs

125 g/1 cup pitted, soft Agen prunes

125 g/1 cup shelled pecans, almonds, hazelnuts or walnuts, or a mixture

150 g/10 tablespoons butter, softened

125 g/½ cup packed light brown soft sugar

175 g/1⅓ cups self-raising flour

1 teaspoon ground cinnamon

3 large eggs, lightly beaten

150 g/1 cup sultanas/golden raisins

juice and zest of 1 orange

juice and zest of 1 unwaxed lemon

2 tablespoons agave nectar (or runny honey)

2 pure cane rough-cut sugar cubes, roughly crushed

an 18-cm/7-in. round pan, 7 cm/3 in. deep , lined with baking parchment and buttered

Serves 12

Preheat the oven to 150°C (300°F) Gas 2.

Using scissors, snip the dried apricots and the prunes into small pieces. Roughly chop the nuts.

Put the butter and sugar in an electric mixer (or use a large mixing bowl and an electric whisk) and beat until combined and fluffy.

Sift the flour and cinnamon into another bowl.

Add the flour mixture and beaten eggs alternately to the butter and sugar, whisking on a low setting all the time.

Using a large metal or wooden spoon, stir in the chopped fruit and nuts, the sultanas/golden raisins, orange and lemon juices and zests and the agave nectar. Mix well.

Tip the mixture into the prepared pan and spread it evenly with a spatula. Sprinkle the crushed sugar over the cake, then bake in the preheated oven for 1¼ hours. Let cool in the pan.

blackcurrant, berry and hazelnut crumble cake

This recipe also works well using damson jam. Either way, treat yourself to some chilled Greek yogurt on the side.

150 g/10 tablespoons butter, softened

175 g/¾ cup (caster) sugar

2 large eggs

125 g/1 cup self-raising flour

50 g/⅓ cup polenta (cornmeal)

1 teaspoon baking powder

finely grated zest of
1 small unwaxed lemon

50 g/¼ cup Greek yogurt

175 g/¾ cup blackcurrant jam

175 g/1¼ cups raspberries

Crumble topping

100 g/⅔ cup shelled, blanched hazelnuts

75 g/⅓ cup demerara sugar

75 g/5 tablespoons butter, chilled and cubed

100 g/¾ cup self-raising flour

a 23-cm/9-in. springform pan, 6 cm/2½ in. deep, lightly buttered and baselined with baking parchment

Serves 12

Preheat the oven to 180°C (350°F) Gas 4.

To make the crumble topping, chop the nuts by hand or pulse them in a food processor – you want them to be roughly chopped. Mix the sugar, butter and flour in an electric mixer until combined, then add 1–2 tablespoons cold water and briefly whiz again until the mixture resembles breadcrumbs. Mix in the nuts. Alternatively, you can rub the butter into the flour by hand in a mixing bowl, then stir in the sugar, water and nuts. Set aside.

Put the butter, sugar, eggs, flour, polenta (cornmeal), baking powder, lemon zest and Greek yogurt in an electric mixer and mix until combined.

Spoon the mixture into the prepared pan and spread it evenly. Tip the jam into a bowl and mix it with a spoon to loosen it, then put spoonfuls over the top of the cake mixture. Using the tip of a round-bladed knife, gently spread the jam by lightly swirling it into the top of the cake mixture. Sprinkle a third of the crumble mixture on top, scatter the raspberries over this, then finish with the remaining crumble topping.

Put the pan on a baking sheet and bake in the preheated oven for 1 hour 5 minutes–1 hour 10 minutes, until just set in the middle. Let cool in the pan before releasing it, removing the base paper and transferring to a plate or board to slice.

mocha swirl cake with espresso icing

The fromage frais in this loaf keeps the fat content down and the polenta gives it a lovely crunchy crust.

1 slightly rounded tablespoon espresso instant coffee powder

1 tablespoon boiling water

200 g/¾ cup fromage frais

75 g/½ cup polenta (cornmeal)

125 g/1 stick butter, softened

225 g/1 cup (caster) sugar

3 large eggs

200 g/1⅗ cups self-raising flour

½ teaspoon bicarbonate of/baking soda

1 teaspoon vanilla extract

2 teaspoons cocoa powder

Espresso icing

100 g/⅔ cup icing/confectioners' sugar

1 slightly rounded teaspoon espresso instant coffee powder

a 19 x 9 x 7-cm/8½ x 4½ x 3-in. loaf pan, lightly buttered and baselined with baking parchment

Serves 8-10

Preheat the oven to 180°C (350°F) Gas 4.

Put the espresso powder and boiling water in a cup and stir to dissolve, then let cool.

Next, take a scant tablespoon from the fromage frais and set it aside for the icing. Put the remaining fromage frais with the polenta (cornmeal), butter, sugar, eggs, flour and bicarbonate of/baking soda in an electric mixer (or use a large mixing bowl and an electric whisk) and beat until combined. Transfer half the mixture to another bowl. Stir the vanilla extract into the first bowl. Stir the dissolved coffee and the cocoa into the second bowl.

Spoon the 2 mixtures into the prepared loaf pan in 3 layers, alternating spoonfuls of each mixture in each layer to resemble a chequerboard. Finally, using a skewer, gently swirl the layers together a few times until you have a definite swirl pattern on top of the loaf.

Bake in the preheated oven for 55 minutes, or until risen and the loaf is a lovely golden colour on top. Let cool in the pan.

To make the espresso icing, sift the icing/confectioners' sugar into a bowl and mix in the espresso powder along with the reserved tablespoon of fromage frais. Add enough cold water to make the icing a spreadable consistency – about 2 teaspoonfuls – but add it gradually, stirring, as you might not need it all.

Run a knife around the edges of the cold loaf in the pan to release it. Turn it out, remove the base paper and spread the icing on top of the loaf. Let set before slicing.

almond cake

This is delicious as is or eaten with baked rhubarb – cut rhubarb into chunks, sprinkle generously with sugar and bake at the same temperature as the cake for 15–20 minutes, or until just soft, then let cool. Buy ready-toasted flaked/slivered almonds to make this cake extra speedy to decorate.

225 g/1 cup (caster) sugar

150 g/10 tablespoons butter, softened and cubed

4 large eggs

1 teaspoon almond extract

75 g/½ cup self-raising flour

1 rounded teaspoon baking powder

125 g/1¼ cups ground almonds

To finish

100 g/⅔ cup icing/confectioners' sugar

freshly squeezed juice of 1 small lemon

2 tablespoons toasted flaked/slivered almonds

an 18-cm/7-in. round, loose-based pan, 7 cm/3 in. deep, lightly buttered and baselined with baking parchment

Serves 8

Preheat the oven to 180°C (350°F) Gas 4.

Put all the ingredients for the cake in an electric mixer (or use a large mixing bowl and an electric whisk) and beat until combined.

Pour the mixture into the prepared pan and spread it evenly with a spatula. Put the pan on a baking sheet and bake in the preheated oven for 40 minutes, or until golden and firm to the touch in the centre. Let the cake cool in the pan.

Tip the cold cake out of the pan and remove the baking parchment. Place on a wire rack over a board.

To finish, sift the icing/confectioners' sugar into a bowl and stir in the lemon juice, little by little. You probably won't need it all – you are aiming for a thick pouring icing. Spoon the icing over the cake, letting it drizzle down the side of the cake. Scatter the flaked/slivered almonds on the top.

crunchy prune and vanilla custard brioche cakes

These individual cakes have an indulgent fruity custard hiding under their crunchy topping. They are also good made with limoncello instead of the brandy, but leave out the alcohol altogether if you prefer. If time is really short, use muffin cases instead of making your own liners. These are best eaten on the day they are made.

2 large eggs

2 tablespoons Armagnac or other brandy

4 tablespoons demerara sugar

½ teaspoon vanilla extract

250 g thick ready-made custard/2 x 4-oz. vanilla pudding snack cups

75 g/5 tablespoons butter

200 g/6½ oz. brioche

100 g/⅔ cup pitted, soft Agen prunes, snipped into small pieces

a 6-hole muffin pan, each hole well buttered and lined with a 17-cm/7-in. square of baking parchment

Makes 6

Preheat the oven to 180°C (350°F) Gas 4.

In a large measuring jug or mixing bowl and using a balloon whisk, whisk together the eggs, Armagnac, 1 tablespoon of the sugar, the vanilla extract and the custard/pudding snacks.

Melt the butter in a small pan and pour into a large mixing bowl.

Cut the brioche into 1–1½-cm/½-inch squares. Toss the squares in the melted butter with 2 tablespoons of the sugar, mixing well. Divide half the squares between the parchment-lined holes in the muffin pan, pressing them down firmly to make a base.

Divide the prune pieces between each muffin, then do the same with the egg mixture. Now add the rest of the brioche squares to the muffins, piling it up high. Scatter the remaining sugar over the top.

Bake in the preheated oven for 35 minutes, or until set and golden on top. Eat warm or cold.

no-bake chocolate, macadamia and fig slices

These are as simple as can be and delicious with an espresso on the side. If you want to make them less sophisticated, for children, you can replace the macadamia nuts with any other type of nut and the dried figs with raisins or dried apricots.

100 g/6½ tablespoons unsalted butter

2 tablespoons (runny) honey

300 g/10 oz. dark/bittersweet chocolate (50–70% cocoa solids), broken into pieces

100 g/3½ oz. milk chocolate, broken into pieces

100 g digestive or other sweetmeal biscuits/ 6 graham crackers

100 g/⅔ cup shelled macadamia nuts

100 g/⅔ cup ready-to-eat dried figs

cocoa powder, for dusting

an 18-cm/7-in. square pan, ideally loose-based, oiled

Makes 16

Put the butter, honey and both types of chocolate in a medium pan and melt gently, stirring from time to time.

Meanwhile, roughly chop the biscuits/crackers, nuts and figs. Stir into the melted chocolate mixture.

Tip the mixture into the prepared pan. Let cool completely before refrigerating for 2–3 hours to set. Cut into 16 slices.

peach, vanilla and cherry shortcake

This is such a pretty option for a summer tea in the garden. Strawberries and raspberries also make a nice topping with a little shredded lemon verbena or, in the autumn, thin slices of baked quince, a handful of blackberries and a scattering of toasted nuts.

100 g/¾ cup plain/
all-purpose flour

75 g/5 tablespoons butter,
softened and cubed

40 g/¼ cup icing/
confectioners' sugar, sifted

1 medium egg yolk

Topping

1 vanilla bean, split
lengthways

125 ml/½ cup double/heavy
or whipping cream, chilled

2 tablespoons icing/
confectioners' sugar, plus
extra for dusting

2 ripe but firm peaches,
pitted and sliced

100 g/1 cup cherries, pitted
and halved

a squeeze of lemon juice

2 tablespoons shredded
basil leaves

*a baking sheet, lined with
baking parchment*

Serves 4

Put the flour, butter, sugar and egg yolk in a food processor and mix together. If the dough doesn't come together, tip it into a bowl and work it with a spatula. Alternatively, you can make it by hand to start with. Tip the dough onto a lightly floured work surface and bring it together in a ball. Press the ball into a disc, wrap in clingfilm/plastic wrap and refrigerate for 15 minutes.

Preheat the oven to 190°C (375°F) Gas 5.

Tip the dough out onto the lightly floured surface and roll or pat it out until it is big enough to cut out a 15-cm/6-inch round – I use a plate or upturned bowl to cut around.

Transfer the round to the prepared baking sheet and bake in the preheated oven for 10–12 minutes, or until set and lightly golden at the edges. Let cool completely.

To make the topping, scrape the seeds out of the vanilla bean and into a bowl with the cream and half the icing/confectioners' sugar. Whip into soft peaks.

Toss the peaches and cherries with the lemon juice, basil and the remaining icing/confectioners' sugar.

Dust the cold shortcake lightly with more icing/confectioners' sugar. Top with the cream mixture and scatter the fruit mixture over the top. Serve immediately.

chocolate snaps with ricotta, pistachios and candied fruit

These are easy but impressive and the flavours are similar to those of Sicilian *cannoli*. For a variation, try moulding some of the baked rounds into tubes – use rounded teaspoonfuls of the mixture and bake in the same way. If you leave the rounds on the baking sheet to cool, as below, they are easy to remove and curl around the base of a wooden spoon or by hand. Bake just a few at a time and fill them with the same ricotta filling.

50 g/3 tablespoons butter

50 g/¼ cup demerara sugar

3 tablespoons golden/corn syrup

40 g/¼ cup plain/all-purpose flour

2 tablespoons cocoa powder, plus extra for dusting

a pinch of salt

Filling

250 g/1 cup ricotta, chilled

1 tablespoon icing/confectioners' sugar

50 g/⅓ cup shelled, unsalted pistachios, finely chopped

50 g/2 oz. dark/bittersweet chocolate (70% cocoa solids), finely chopped

25 g/⅙ cup chopped mixed candied peel

1 teaspoon orange flower water

a large baking sheet, lined with baking parchment

Makes 10

Heat the butter, sugar and golden/corn syrup together in a small pan until the butter has melted and the sugar dissolved, stirring every now and then. Pour into a mixing bowl. Sift in the flour, cocoa and salt, mix thoroughly and let cool for 15 minutes.

Preheat the oven to 160°C (325°F) Gas 3.

Drop 10 teaspoonfuls of the chocolate mixture onto the prepared baking sheet. Leave about 6–7 cm/2½ inches between them to allow the snaps to spread as they bake. Flatten them very slightly with the back of the teaspoon before baking in the preheated oven for 8 minutes. Let cool on the baking sheet for 3–4 minutes before transferring to a wire rack to cool completely and become crisp – this will take only a matter of minutes.

Repeat with the second half of the mixture so that you end up with 20 rounds in total.

To make the filling, mix all the ingredients together in a bowl. Generously sandwich the snaps together with the filling. Lightly dust the top of each one with cocoa.

pear, mascarpone and orange tarts

Using ready-made and ready-rolled puff pastry makes life easy here. Slices of plum or dessert apple would also work well as a topping for these tarts.

300 g/10 oz. chilled ready-made, ready-rolled puff pastry

40 g/3 tablespoons butter

125 g/½ cup mascarpone

3 tablespoons (caster) sugar, plus extra for sprinkling

finely grated zest of 1 small orange

75 g/¾ cup ground almonds

1 large egg yolk

4 ripe but firm small pears, cored and thinly sliced (no need to peel)

3–4 tablespoons smooth apricot jam

4 tablespoons toasted flaked/slivered almonds

2–3 large baking sheets, lined with baking parchment and oiled

Makes 12

Preheat the oven to 220°C (425°F) Gas 7.

Take the pastry out of the fridge.

Melt the butter in a small pan and let cool slightly.

Put the mascarpone, sugar, orange zest, ground almonds and egg yolk in a bowl and mix. Refrigerate until needed.

Halve the pastry and roll one half out on a lightly floured work surface until it is about 2 mm/⅟₁₆ inch – any thicker than that and the pastry won't crisp up in the oven. Trim the edges with a sharp knife to make a 21 x 24-cm/9 x 10-inch piece, then cut that into six 7 x 12-cm/3 x 5-inch rectangles. Arrange the rectangles on one of the prepared baking sheets.

Repeat with the other half of the pastry.

Brush the edges of each rectangle with the melted butter and sprinkle a little sugar over them. Put 2 teaspoons of the mascarpone mixture in the centre of each rectangle. Spread the mixture out using a small knife, leaving a border of about 1 cm/⅜ inch all the way round.

Top each tart with overlapping slices of pear and scatter a little more sugar over the top. Bake the tarts in the preheated oven for 15 minutes, or until the pastry is golden and crisp. Transfer to a wire rack.

Warm the apricot jam in a small pan, then use to brush over the pear slices. Sprinkle the flaked/slivered almonds over the top, then let cool.

fill the tins

zucchini, carrot and pear cake with poppy seed frosting

200 g/1½ cups plain/all-purpose flour

100 g/¾ cup spelt flour

1 teaspoon baking powder

1 teaspoon bicarbonate of/baking soda

1 tablespoon ground cinnamon

2 pinches of ground cloves

4 large eggs

275 g/1⅓ cups light muscovado or packed light brown soft sugar

250 ml/1 cup virgin coconut oil or rapeseed/canola oil

150 g/1 cup grated carrots

100 g/⅔ cup grated courgettes/zucchini

2 pears, cored and chopped

150 g/1 cup walnut or pecan pieces

100 g/⅔ cup sultanas/golden raisins

Poppy seed frosting

75 g/5 tablespoons unsalted butter, very soft

200 g/6½ oz. cream cheese, chilled

100 g/⅓ cup Greek yogurt, chilled

175 g/1¼ cups icing/confectioners' sugar, sifted

1 tablespoon poppy seeds

two 20-cm/8-in. round cake pans, buttered and base-lined with baking parchment

Serves 12

Coconut oil often solidifies in its container, so immerse the pot or jar in a bowl of hot water, from the kettle, for about 10 minutes to melt the oil. To make this cake completely dairy-free, replace the butter, cream cheese and yogurt in the frosting with 200 g/6½ oz. soy cream cheese, sweetened with 2 tablespoons icing/confectioners' sugar. This cake will store well for a few days, but even longer if kept in an airtight container in the fridge. Serve it at room temperature.

Preheat the oven to 180°C (350°F) Gas 4.

Sift the flours, baking powder and bicarbonate of/baking soda into the bowl of an electric mixer (or use a large mixing bowl and an electric whisk). Tip any spelt left in the sieve/strainer into the bowl too. Add the cinnamon, cloves, eggs, sugar and oil. Mix together.

In another bowl, mix the carrots, courgettes/zucchini, pears, nuts and sultanas/golden raisins. Using a large metal spoon, fold these ingredients into the cake mixture, making sure everything is thoroughly combined.

Divide the mixture between the prepared pans and spread it evenly with a spatula. Bake in the preheated oven for 40–45 minutes, or until risen, golden and set in the centre. Let cool in the pans.

To make the poppy seed frosting, whisk together the butter and cream cheese, add the yogurt and icing/confectioners' sugar and whisk again – an electric whisk makes quick work of this. Stir in the poppy seeds, then refrigerate until needed.

Tip the cold cakes out of the pans and peel off the base papers. Place one cake on a board or serving plate, bottom-side uppermost. Spread half the frosting over it. Put the other cake on top, top-side uppermost, and spread the remaining frosting over the top.

tropical chai pineapple cake

200 ml/¾ cup boiling water

3 chai tea bags

350 g/12 oz. prepared fresh pineapple

250 g/8 oz. mixed soft dried tropical fruit, e.g. pineapple, papaya, mango, melon

100 g/3½ oz. pitted, soft dates

150 g/1 cup raisins

125 g/⅔ cup dark muscovado or packed dark brown soft sugar

1 teaspoon bicarbonate of/baking soda

1 tablespoon ground allspice

1 teaspoon freshly grated nutmeg

1 small cinnamon stick

3 star anise

4 tablespoons dark rum

150 g/10 tablespoons butter, chopped

grated zest of 2 limes

125 g/1 cup plain/all-purpose flour

125 g/1 cup self-raising flour

100 g/⅔ cup shelled brazil nuts, chopped

2 large eggs, lightly beaten

3 tablespoons (runny) honey

dried pineapple slices, to decorate

a 20-cm/8-in. round pan, 9 cm/4 in. deep, lightly buttered and baselined with baking parchment

Serves 16

This soft-textured, moist fruit cake keeps for up to two weeks and is flavoured with chai tea, which has warm undertones of cinnamon and ginger. If you can't find soft dried tropical fruit, use ready-to-eat dried apricots, pears, apples, peaches or prunes, or a mixture, instead.

Pour the boiling water into a measuring jug/cup, add the tea bags, stir and set aside while you prepare the rest of the ingredients.

Chop the pineapple into small pieces and set aside.

Chop the dried fruit and the dates into small chunks. Put into a medium pan with the raisins, sugar, bicarbonate of/baking soda, all the spices, the rum and butter. Discard the tea bags from the chai tea and pour that into the pan too. Stir together and bring the mixture to simmering point over gentle heat.

When the butter has melted, increase the heat and boil the mixture for 2 minutes exactly, then transfer the contents to a large mixing bowl. Stir in the pineapple and lime zest and let cool completely, giving it a stir from time to time, as and when you remember.

Preheat the oven to 160°C (325°F) Gas 3.

Remove the cinnamon stick and star anise from the mixture. Sift both flours into the bowl and add the chopped nuts and beaten eggs. Stir well.

Tip the mixture into the prepared pan and spread it evenly with a spatula. Bake in the preheated oven for 1¾ hours, or until risen and deep golden brown. Let cool in the pan.

Tip the cold cake out of the pan and peel off the base paper. Warm the honey in a small pan, then use to brush all over the cake. Decorate with dried pineapple slices.

banana and passion-fruit cake

For the best flavour, make sure your bananas are really ripe for this, even if they are at the stage when they have turned black in the fruit bowl and no one wants to eat them; they will be perfect to use in this cake.

225 g/1¾ cups self-raising flour

½ teaspoon bicarbonate of/baking soda

100 g/6½ tablespoons butter, softened and cubed

175 g/¾ cup (caster) sugar

2 large eggs, lightly beaten

3 passion fruit

3 very ripe bananas

To decorate

100 g/⅝ cup icing/confectioners' sugar

1 passion fruit

dried banana slices, to decorate

a 19 x 9 x 7-cm/8½ x 4½ x 3-in. loaf pan, lightly buttered and baselined with baking parchment

Serves 8-10

Preheat the oven to 180°C (350°F) Gas 4.

Sift the flour and bicarbonate of/baking soda into a bowl. Put the butter and sugar in an electric mixer (or use a large mixing bowl and an electric whisk) and beat until pale and fluffy. Add the beaten eggs and sifted flour mixture alternately to the bowl.

Halve the passion fruit and scoop out the pulp into a sieve/strainer over a bowl. Using a teaspoon, press and stir the pulp to extract the juice. Discard the leftover seeds. Peel and mash the bananas. Add the passion-fruit pulp and mashed banana to the cake mixture and mix again.

Tip the mixture into the prepared loaf pan and spread it evenly with a spatula. Bake in the preheated oven for 55 minutes, or until golden and risen. Let cool in the pan.

To decorate, sift the icing/confectioners' sugar into a small bowl. Halve the passion fruit and scoop out the pulp into the bowl – no need to sieve/strain the pulp this time. Mix together with a teaspoon. The glaze will seem stiff at first, but persevere until is thoroughly mixed. If the glaze still seems a little thick, add a drop or two of cold water – the consistency will depend on the size of the passion fruit and how ripe it is. You want the glaze to be a thick, spreadable consistency.

Tip the cold cake out of the pan and peel off the base paper. Spoon the glaze over the top of the cake and decorate with dried banana slices. Let set for about 30 minutes before slicing.

sticky-topped marmalade and ginger loaf

This loaf keeps really well in a tin or airtight container for several days. It freezes well too, but add the marmalade topping after defrosting. This is a good one to slice and take on picnics or wintry walks.

125 g/1 stick butter, softened and cubed

125 g/½ cup dark muscovado or packed dark brown soft sugar

200 g/1⅔ cups plain/all-purpose flour, sifted

2 teaspoons baking powder

1 teaspoon ground ginger

2 large eggs, lightly beaten with 150 ml/⅔ cup milk

4 tablespoons black treacle/blackstrap molasses

5 tablespoons orange medium-cut marmalade

3 balls stem ginger in syrup, drained and finely chopped

100 g/⅔ cup ready-to-eat dried apricots, snipped into small pieces

a 19 x 9 x 7-cm/8½ x 4½ x 3-in. loaf pan, lightly buttered and baselined with baking parchment

Serves 8-10

Preheat the oven to 190°C (375°F) Gas 5.

Put the butter and sugar in an electric mixer (or use a large mixing bowl and an electric whisk) and beat until combined. Tip in the flour, baking powder and ground ginger and add the egg mixture and black treacle/molasses. Mix everything together. Stir in 3 tablespoons of the marmalade, the chopped ginger and the apricots.

Tip the mixture into the prepared pan and bake in the preheated oven for 50 minutes–1 hour or until risen and set. Let cool in the pan. Towards the end of cooling, gently heat the remaining marmalade and spread it over the top of the loaf. Let cool completely before carefully tipping the loaf out of the pan and peeling off the base paper.

apple and amaretto cake

This cake is quick to make and can be left to bake while you get on with other things. It freezes well and is delicious as is; for added indulgence, whipped cream mixed with a little icing/confectioners' sugar and almond-flavoured Amaretto makes a heavenly accompaniment.

450 g/1 lb. dessert apples

350 g/2⅔ cups plain/
all-purpose flour, sifted

1 tablespoon baking powder

2 teaspoons ground
cinnamon

200 g/14 tablespoons butter,
softened and cubed

150 g/¾ cup light muscovado
or packed light brown soft
sugar

2 large eggs

100 ml/⅓ cup milk

100 ml/⅓ cup Amaretto

200 g/1⅓ cups sultanas/
golden raisins

To decorate

3 small, red-skinned dessert
apples

2 tablespoons (runny) honey

*a 23-cm/9-in. springform
pan, 6 cm/2½ in. deep, lightly
buttered and baselined with
baking parchment*

Serves 8–10

Preheat the oven to 180°C (350°F) Gas 4.

Core, peel and chop the apples into equal 1-cm/½-inch chunks.

Tip the flour, baking powder, cinnamon, butter, sugar, eggs, milk and Amaretto into the bowl of an electric mixer (or use a large mixing bowl and an electric whisk) and beat together until combined.

Using a large metal spoon, thoroughly stir in the chopped apples and the sultanas/golden raisins.

Spoon the mixture into the prepared pan and spread it evenly with a spatula.

To decorate, quarter the 3 red-skinned dessert apples. Don't peel them, but core them and thinly slice the quarters. Arrange the slices, slightly overlapping, on top of the cake in concentric circles.

Put the pan on a baking sheet and bake in the preheated oven for 1½–1¾ hours, or until risen and golden and the apple slices on top are burnished. Cover the cake with foil towards the end of cooking to prevent over-browning, if necessary.

Warm the honey in a small pan, then use to brush over the top of the cake. Let cool in the pan before releasing it, peeling off the base paper and transferring to a plate or board to slice.

back-from-school traffic-light jam tarts

A goodie to have in the house for children when they return from school, starving, at teatime.

300 g/10 oz. ready-made shortcrust pastry

100–125 g/⅓–½ cup each raspberry, apricot and greengage jam

a little beaten egg, for brushing (optional)

a plain or fluted 8–9-cm/3½-in. cookie cutter

a 12-hole shallow bun pan, oiled

Makes 12

On a lightly floured work surface, roll out the pastry until it is about 2–3 mm/⅛ inch thick. It may be easier to roll out half at a time. Using the cutter, stamp out 12 rounds and use to line the holes of the pan. Reserve the pastry trimmings. Chill the pastry-lined pan for 30 minutes.

Preheat the oven to 200°C (400°F) Gas 6.

Put about 2 teaspoonfuls of raspberry jam in 4 of the pastry cases, apricot jam in another 4 and greengage jam in the rest. Don't overfill them, otherwise the jam will bubble over the sides while they are cooking.

Re-roll the pastry trimmings and cut out short, thin strips of pastry. Place 2 parallel strips on top of each tart, twisting the strips as you do so and trimming them to fit the tarts. Press down the ends. Now place 2 more parallel strips at right angles to the first pair to create a lattice effect. Brush the lattice with a little beaten egg, if you like – it helps the pastry to brown.

Bake in the preheated oven for 20 minutes. Let cool for 5 minutes, then transfer to a rack to cool completely.

honey, toasted pine nut and pumpkin-seed flapjacks with chocolate topping

Vary the dried fruit you use in these flapjacks according to what you have handy. They are a hit with children and adults alike.

3 tablespoons pine nuts

2 tablespoons pumpkin seeds

175 g/1½ sticks butter

100 g/½ cup packed light brown soft sugar

3 tablespoons (runny) honey

100 g/⅔ cup dried sour cherries or cranberries, or chopped ready-to-eat dried apricots, pears, peaches or prunes, or a mixture

250 g/2 cups porridge oats

a pinch of salt

200 g/6½ oz. milk chocolate, broken into pieces

a 20-cm/8-in. square, loose-based pan, lightly buttered

Makes 24

Preheat the oven to 180°C (350°F) Gas 4.

Spread the pine nuts and pumpkin seeds on a baking sheet and toast in the preheated oven for 5 minutes, or until lightly golden. Let cool, then roughly chop.

Gently heat the butter, sugar and honey together in a small pan until melted, stirring every now and then. Remove the pan from the heat and let cool slightly.

Tip the dried fruit and oats into a large mixing bowl. Add the salt and the chopped pine nuts and seeds. Pour in the warm butter mixture and mix well.

Tip the mixture into the prepared pan and press down firmly with the back of a spoon to make an even layer. Put the pan on a baking sheet. Bake in the preheated oven for 30 minutes, or until lightly golden.

Meanwhile, melt the chocolate in a heatproof bowl set over a pan of barely simmering water. Pour over the flapjack, then let cool completely.

Remove the flapjack from the pan and cut into 24 bars.

really lemony gluten-free cake

The lemon zest and juice make this cake lovely and moist, and it will keep in an airtight tin for several days – store it whole and cut it as needed.

200 g/14 tablespoons butter, softened

200 g/1 cup (caster) sugar

4 large eggs

150 g/1 generous cup gluten-free self-raising white flour blend, sifted

2 teaspoons gluten-free baking powder

50 g/⅓ cup polenta (cornmeal)

finely grated zest and juice of 1 lemon

Lemon syrup

75 g/½ cup icing/confectioners' sugar

finely grated zest and freshly squeezed juice of 3 lemons

Candied lemons

250 g/1¼ cups (caster) sugar

2 lemons

an 18-cm/8-in. square pan, 6 cm/2½ in. deep, lightly buttered and baselined with baking parchment

Serves 16

Preheat the oven to 180°C (350°F) Gas 4.

Put the butter, sugar, eggs, flour, baking powder, polenta (cornmeal) and lemon zest and juice in an electric mixer (or use a large mixing bowl and an electric whisk) and beat until combined. Spoon the mixture into the prepared pan. Bake in the preheated oven for 45 minutes, or until risen, firm to the touch and golden.

Meanwhile, to make the lemon syrup, sift the icing/confectioners' sugar into a bowl and whisk in the lemon zest and juice with a balloon whisk. Set aside to allow the sugar to dissolve.

To make the candied lemons, put the sugar and 250 ml/1 cup water into a pan. Gently heat, stirring, until the sugar has dissolved. Slice the lemons and flick out as many of the pips as you can. Add the lemon slices to the liquid in the pan – you want the lemons to cook more or less in a single layer. Bring to a simmer, then gently cook, uncovered, for 45 minutes, stirring from time to time.

When the cake is ready, take it out of the oven and make holes all over the surface with a fork. Spoon the lemon syrup over the cake, allowing it to seep in between spoonfuls – it will seem like a lot, but gluten-free flour is very absorbent. Let the cake and candied lemons cool completely.

Turn the cake out of the pan and arrange the candied lemons on top, discarding the liquid they were cooked in.

hazelnut, orange and marsala raisin biscotti

Biscotti are crunchy Italian double-baked cookies and they will keep for a month or so, making them a great standby. Dip the biscotti into Vin Santo, limoncello, tea or a good espresso, as you eat them.

100 g/⅔ cup raisins

2 tablespoons Marsala

250 g/2 cups self-raising flour

3 tablespoons cocoa powder

1 teaspoon baking powder

150 g/¾ cup (caster) sugar

2 large eggs, lightly beaten

finely grated zest of 1 large orange

100 g/⅔ cup blanched hazelnuts, roughly chopped

2 baking sheets, lined with baking parchment

Makes about 30

Preheat the oven to 180°C (350°F) Gas 4.

Put the raisins in a small bowl with the Marsala, stir and let soak for at least 15 minutes.

Tip the flour, cocoa, baking powder and sugar into a food processor and whiz to mix. Add the beaten eggs and orange zest and whiz again for a couple of minutes until the mixture resembles coarse breadcrumbs. Tip the mixture into a mixing bowl and add the raisins and their liquid, and the chopped hazelnuts.

Using a spatula or wooden spoon, mix and knead everything together in the bowl until it starts to clump together – this will take a few minutes. Tip the dough out onto a lightly floured work surface and bring together into a ball with your hands.

Halve the dough and briefly knead each half. Roll each one into a 20-cm/8-inch long log. Put both logs onto one of the prepared baking sheets, leaving about 8–10 cm/ 4 inches between them to allow them to spread as they bake. Bake in the preheated oven for 35 minutes.

Remove the baked logs from the oven and let cool for 15 minutes, or until they are cool enough to handle. Meanwhile, reduce the oven temperature to 150°C (300°F) Gas 3.

Using a serrated bread knife, slice the logs on the diagonal into 1-cm/⅜-inch-thick slices. You should get about 15 slices from each log. Discard the ends.

Arrange the slices on the 2 baking sheets in a single layer and bake them for a further 20 minutes to dry them out. Let cool on wire racks.

special
occasions

mulled wine and cranberry tea bread

This bread is studded with juicy fruit and nuts, perfect for autumn and winter. It is delicious sliced and eaten as it is or spread with unsalted butter.

a wine-mulling spice bag

200 ml/¾ cup light, fruity red wine

1 tablespoon (runny) honey

75 g/⅓ cup ready-to-eat dried figs

50 g/⅓ cup crystallized stem ginger

75 g/½ cup whole blanched almonds

50 g/⅓ cup each dried cranberries and dried sour cherries

100 g/½ cup light muscovado or packed light brown soft sugar

2 large eggs, lightly beaten

grated zest of 2 oranges

100 g/1 cup fresh cranberries

225 g/1¾ cups self-raising flour

1 teaspoon ground cinnamon

½ teaspoon ground allspice

Topping

75 g/½ cup dried cranberries (or dried sour cherries)

2 tablespoons orange juice

4 tablespoons redcurrant jelly

a 19 x 9 x 7-cm/8½ x 4½ x 3-in. loaf pan, lightly buttered and baselined with baking parchment

Serves 12

First make the mulled wine. Put the wine-mulling spice bag in a medium pan with the red wine and honey. Slowly bring to a simmer, stirring now and then. Leave over very low heat for 5 minutes, then take the pan off the heat and set aside.

Roughly chop the figs, ginger and almonds and mix with the dried cranberries and cherries and the sugar in a mixing bowl. Remove the spice bag from the mulled wine, then pour the warm wine over the dried fruit and let soak for 30 minutes.

Preheat the oven to 160°C (325°F) Gas 3.

Stir the beaten eggs, orange zest and the fresh cranberries into the soaked dried fruit. Next, sift in the flour, cinnamon and allspice. Mix together until thoroughly combined.

Spoon the mixture into the prepared loaf pan. Bake in the preheated oven for 55 minutes, by which time the loaf will have risen and slightly shrunk from the sides of the pan. Let cool in the pan, then run a table knife around the edge of the pan, tip the loaf out and peel off the base paper.

To make the topping, gently heat the cranberries, orange juice and redcurrant jelly in a small pan over low heat, stirring until the jelly has dissolved.

Brush the top of the loaf with some of the sticky juices from the topping, then spoon the cranberries along the centre of the loaf. Let cool before serving.

snowman cookies

These are fun to make with children. If you don't want to have to buy three types of coloured icing, use red for both the noses and the mouths – or tiny pieces of candied peel also make fine snowman noses.

225 g/1¾ cups self-raising flour, sifted

100 g/6½ tablespoons butter, softened

100 g/½ cup packed light brown soft sugar

1 large egg

1 tablespoon golden/corn syrup

a pinch of ground cinnamon (optional)

To decorate

icing/confectioners' sugar, for dusting

400 g/14 oz. ready-to-roll white icing

2 teaspoons golden/corn syrup

24 currants, halved

about 50 g/2 oz. ready-to-roll orange icing

about 50 g/2 oz. ready-to-roll red icing

150 g/6 oz. ready-to-roll black, blue or green icing

a plain 7-cm/3-in. cookie cutter

2 baking sheets, oiled

Makes 24

Put the flour, butter, sugar, egg, golden/corn syrup and cinnamon, if using, in the bowl of an electric mixer and beat together until combined. Bring the dough together with your hands, then wrap in clingfilm/plastic wrap and refrigerate for 1 hour or longer – even overnight is fine, if you want to get ahead.

Preheat the oven to 180°C (350°F) Gas 4.

Tip half the dough out onto a lightly floured work surface and roll out until it is 4–5 mm/³⁄₁₆ inch thick. Using the cutter, stamp out 12 rounds and arrange them on the baking sheets. Bake in the preheated oven for 10–12 minutes, or until lightly golden. Let cool on wire racks.

Repeat with the other half of the dough.

To decorate, lightly dust the work surface and a rolling pin with icing/confectioners' sugar. Roll out half the white icing until it is 3 mm/⅛ inch thick. Using the cutter again, stamp out 12 rounds. Repeat with the other half of the icing.

Put a dab of golden/corn syrup in the centre of each cookie to act as glue and place a round of white icing on each one. Make 2 eyes on each snowman by pressing 2 currant halves into the icing quite firmly.

Next, using your hands, roll 24 small, carrot-shaped noses from the orange icing, making indentations along the length of each one with a small knife. Stick the noses onto the snowman faces with the tiniest dab of water.

Roll the red icing into 24 short, thin strips and pinch the ends. Stick one to each face for a mouth.

Using a rolling pin again, roll out the black, blue or green icing, in batches, and cut out hat shapes. Make indentations for the brims. Stick the hats on, then let the snowmen dry for an hour or so before serving.

ultimate chocolate fudge cake with honeycomb

If you want to get ahead, you can freeze the filled and topped cake, then defrost and sprinkle with the honeycomb/sponge candy to serve.

2 tablespoons cocoa powder

3 tablespoons boiling water

225 g/1¾ cups self-raising flour

2 teaspoons baking powder

200 g/14 tablespoons butter, softened

250 g/1¼ cups light muscovado or packed light brown soft sugar

2 tablespoons crème fraîche

1 teaspoon vanilla extract

4 large eggs, lightly beaten

Honeycomb/sponge candy

75 g/⅓ cup (caster) sugar

2 tablespoons golden/corn syrup

1 tablespoon bicarbonate of/baking soda

Chocolate fudge frosting

200 g/6½ oz. dark/bittersweet chocolate (about 50% cocoa solids), broken into pieces

175 g/⅔ cup crème fraîche

1 tablespoon vegetable oil

two 20-cm/8-in. round cake pans, lightly buttered and baselined with baking parchment

a baking sheet, lined with baking parchment

Serves 8

Preheat the oven to 180°C (350°F) Gas 4.

Dissolve the cocoa in the boiling water, then let cool. Sift the flour and baking powder into a bowl.

Put the butter and sugar in an electric mixer (or use a large mixing bowl and an electric whisk) and beat for 3–4 minutes, or until smooth and fluffy. Mix in the crème fraîche, vanilla extract and the cooled, dissolved cocoa. With the mixer running on a slow speed, add the beaten eggs and sifted flour mixture alternately to the bowl.

Divide the mixture between the prepared pans and spread it evenly with a spatula. Bake in the preheated oven for 25–30 minutes, or until firm to the touch. Let cool in the pans for 30 minutes. Tip out onto a wire rack and peel off the base papers. Let cool completely.

To make the honeycomb/sponge candy, put the sugar and golden/corn syrup in a medium pan over gentle heat. Heat, stirring, until the sugar has melted. Increase the heat and bubble for 1 minute exactly. Take the pan off the heat and quickly stir in the bicarbonate of/baking soda – the mixture will go white and frothy. Immediately pour it onto the prepared baking sheet and let cool to set.

To make the chocolate fudge frosting, put all the ingredients in a heatproof bowl over a pan of barely simmering water and leave until smooth and glossy, stirring now and then. Take the bowl off the pan and let cool.

To assemble, place one cake on a board or large serving plate and spread about a third of the chocolate fudge frosting over the top. Place the other cake on top and coat entirely in the rest of the frosting. Chop the honeycomb/sponge candy into chunks and sprinkle on top of the cake – any leftovers are a cook's perk!

rosewater, pistachio and grapefruit cake

You can buy crystallized pink rose petals in jars, or, to make your own, dip unsprayed petals in lightly beaten egg white followed by granulated sugar. Shake off the excess sugar, then let the petals dry on baking parchment until crisp. Serve the cake with Greek yogurt sweetened with a little honey.

200 g/1⅓ cups shelled, unsalted pistachios

200 g/1⅓ cups self-raising flour

1 tablespoon bicarbonate of/baking soda

150 g/10 tablespoons butter, softened and cubed

150 g/¾ cup (caster) sugar

3 large eggs, lightly beaten

2 tablespoons rosewater

4 tablespoons buttermilk

grated zest of 2 pink or red grapefruit

a few crystallized rose petals, to decorate

Grapefruit syrup

1 pink or red grapefruit

1 tablespoon rosewater

75 g/⅓ cup (caster) sugar

a 23-cm/9-in. springform pan, 6 cm/2½ in. deep, lightly buttered

Serves 10–12

Preheat the oven to 180°C (350°F) Gas 4.

Begin by whizzing 150 g/1 cup of the pistachios in a food processor until finely ground. Roughly chop the remaining 50 g/⅓ cup and mix three-quarters of them with the ground pistachios. Reserve the rest for scattering on the cake to decorate.

Sift the flour and bicarbonate of/baking soda into the bowl of an electric mixer. Add the butter and mix together, on the lowest speed, until the mixture resembles clumpy breadcrumbs. Add the pistachios, sugar, beaten eggs, rosewater, buttermilk and grapefruit zest and mix until combined. The mixture will be thick, so you will probably need to stop a couple of times to scrape the mixture off the paddle.

Tip the mixture into prepared pan and spread it evenly with a spatula. Bake in the preheated oven for about 45 minutes, or until golden and risen.

Towards the end of the cooking time, make the grapefruit syrup. Squeeze the juice of the grapefruit through a sieve/strainer and into a medium pan. Add the rosewater and sugar to the pan and gently heat together, stirring, until the sugar has dissolved. Increase the heat and boil for 2 minutes to make the liquid slightly more syrupy.

When the cake is ready, remove it from the oven and, using a small, fine skewer, make a few holes over the surface of the cake. Spoon over the warm grapefruit syrup, allowing it to seep in between spoonfuls. Let the cake cool completely in its pan.

Once cold, pop the cake out of the pan and scatter the reserved chopped pistachios and a few crystallized rose petals on top.

victoria sandwich with fresh mint and strawberries

The cake layers for this classic English recipe are best eaten as fresh as possible. They are also delicious sandwiched together with good-quality raspberry jam or a citrus curd and some whipped cream.

200 g/14 tablespoons unsalted butter, softened

200 g/1 cup (caster) sugar

4 large eggs, lightly beaten

1 teaspoon vanilla extract

200 g/1⅔ cups self-raising flour, sifted

2 teaspoons baking powder

a pinch of salt

icing/confectioners' sugar, for dusting

Filling

250 g/1 pint ripe strawberries

2 tablespoons icing/confectioners' sugar

grated zest of 1 unwaxed lemon

150 g/⅔ cup crème fraîche or double/heavy cream, chilled

100 g/⅓ cup mascarpone, chilled

1 tablespoon shredded mint leaves

two 20-cm/8-in. round cake pans, lightly buttered and baselined with baking parchment

Serves 8

Preheat the oven to 180°C (350°F) Gas 4.

Put the butter and sugar in an electric mixer (or use a large mixing bowl and an electric whisk) and beat for 3–4 minutes, or until pale and fluffy. Gradually add the beaten eggs with the beaters still running, followed by the vanilla extract, flour, baking powder and salt. Mix until all the ingredients are combined.

Divide the mixture between the prepared pans and spread it evenly with a spatula. Bake in the preheated oven for 25 minutes, or until lightly golden and risen. Let cool in the pans for 30 minutes. Tip the cakes out onto a wire rack and peel off the base papers. Let cool completely.

To make the filling, hull and thinly slice the strawberries, then mix in a bowl with half the icing/confectioners' sugar and all the lemon zest. Let macerate for up to 30 minutes.

In another bowl, use a balloon whisk to whisk the crème fraîche or cream and mascarpone together until smooth. Stir in the rest of the icing/confectioners' sugar and the shredded mint.

To assemble, place one cake on a board or large serving plate and spread the creamy filling over the top. Scatter the strawberries over the filling. Place the other cake on top and dust with icing/confectioners' sugar.

white chocolate and apricot roulade

This summer stunner, once assembled, will hold for a couple of hours before serving – keep it in a cool place, but not the fridge. To make it look extra special, use a vegetable peeler to make curls from a block of white chocolate to scatter on top.

4 large eggs

100 g/½ cup (caster) sugar

2 pinches of saffron threads

100 g/¾ cup self-raising flour, sifted

3 tablespoons flaked/slivered almonds

1 tablespoon icing/confectioners' sugar, plus extra for dusting

Apricot filling

seeds from 4 cardamom pods, crushed

1 tablespoon orange blossom honey or other (runny) honey

1 tablespoon freshly squeezed lemon juice

8 apricots, pitted and finely chopped

White chocolate cream

75 g/2½ oz. white chocolate, broken into pieces, plus extra if making curls

175 g/⅔ cup crème fraîche

200 ml/¾ cup double/heavy cream

a 24 x 37-cm/9 x 14-in. Swiss/jelly roll pan, 2.5 cm/1 in. deep, oiled and baselined with baking parchment

Serves 10-12

Preheat the oven to 190°C (375°F) Gas 5.

Break the eggs into a large heatproof mixing bowl and add the sugar and saffron. Place over a pan of simmering water, making sure the base doesn't touch the water. Using an electric whisk, whisk the ingredients for 5 minutes, or until pale and voluminous. Take the bowl off the heat. Using a large metal spoon, carefully fold the flour into the mixture.

Tip the mixture into the prepared pan and gently spread it evenly with a spatula. Sprinkle the flaked/slivered almonds over the top. Bake in the preheated oven for 12–15 minutes, or until lightly golden. Meanwhile, cover a large board with a sheet of baking parchment and sift the tablespoon of icing/confectioners' sugar evenly over it.

When the cake is ready, let it settle, out of the oven, for 10 minutes. Run a small, sharp knife around the edges before turning it upside down over the sugared parchment. Remove the pan and peel off the base paper. Roll up the cake from one of the shorter ends, rolling the sugared parchment with it as you do so – you may need to make a cut along the width of the cake about an inch in, to help you start rolling. Let cool completely.

To make the apricot filling, put all the ingredients in a pan and simmer gently, uncovered, for 10 minutes – you want the apricots to be soft, but still retaining their shape. Let cool, then refrigerate until needed.

To make the white chocolate cream, put the chocolate and 2 tablespoons of the crème fraîche in a small heatproof bowl over a pan of barely simmering water. Leave until melted, stirring from time to time. Take the bowl off the heat and let cool slightly. Whisk the cream in a bowl until it forms soft peaks, then stir in the remaining crème fraîche and the cooled chocolate mixture.

Unroll the cake onto a board. Spread the white chocolate cream over it and scatter the apricot mixture on top. Roll up the roulade and dust with icing/confectioners' sugar.

cinnamon blueberry cake

Make this cake on the day you are going to eat it, but let it cool completely before assembling and serving.

175 g/1½ sticks unsalted butter, softened

175 g/¾ cup (caster) sugar

4 large eggs, lightly beaten

a pinch of ground cinnamon

175 g/1⅓ cups self-raising flour, sifted

2 teaspoons baking powder

a pinch of salt

225 g/1 pint blueberries

Cinnamon frosting

200 g/6½ oz. cream cheese, chilled

100 g/scant ½ cup crème fraîche or double/heavy cream, chilled

50 g/3 tablespoons unsalted butter, softened and cubed

150 g/1 cup icing/confectioners' sugar, sifted, plus extra for dusting

2 teaspoons ground cinnamon

two 20-cm/8-in. round cake pans, lightly buttered and baselined with baking parchment

Serves 8

Preheat the oven to 180°C (350°F) Gas 4.

Put the butter and sugar in an electric mixer (or use a large mixing bowl and an electric whisk) and beat for 3–4 minutes, or until pale and fluffy. Gradually add the beaten eggs with the beaters still running, followed by the cinnamon, flour, baking powder and salt. Mix until all the ingredients are combined.

Divide the mixture between the prepared pans and spread it evenly with a spatula. Bake in the preheated oven for 20–25 minutes, or until lightly golden and risen. Let cool in the pans for 30 minutes. Tip the cakes out onto a wire rack and peel off the base papers. Let cool completely.

To make the cinnamon frosting, whisk all the ingredients together to combine.

To assemble, place one cake on a cake stand or large serving plate and spread two-thirds of the cinnamon frosting over the top – a spatula or table knife is the ideal tool to use here. Scatter three-quarters of the blueberries on top of the frosting.

Place the other cake on the blueberries and spread the remaining frosting over the top. Finish with the rest of the blueberries. Dust with a little icing/confectioners' sugar.

chocolate chestnut brownie torte

This torte has the texture of a brownie, but it is as light as a feather. It doesn't contain any flour, which is an added bonus for anyone with an intolerance to wheat. In addition to being dusted with cocoa, it also looks pretty scattered with chopped *marrons glacés* – candied chestnuts.

200 g/6½ oz. dark/bittersweet chocolate (70% cocoa solids), broken into pieces

175 g/1½ sticks unsalted butter, cubed

5 large eggs, separated

175 g/¾ cup (caster) sugar

a pinch of salt

100 g/3½ oz. canned unsweetened chestnut purée

cocoa powder, for dusting

a few chopped, toasted hazelnuts, to decorate

a 23-cm/9-in. springform pan, 6 cm/2½ in. deep, oiled and baselined with baking parchment

Serves 8

Preheat the oven to 180°C (350°F) Gas 4.

Put the chocolate and butter in a heatproof bowl set over a pan of barely simmering water. Stir until the chocolate has melted and the mixture is smooth and glossy. Take the bowl off the heat and let cool slightly.

Put the egg yolks, 100 g/½ cup of the sugar and the salt in the bowl of an electric mixer (or use a large mixing bowl and an electric whisk) and beat until pale and mousse-like – about 5 minutes. Mash and stir the chestnut purée with the back of a spoon in a small bowl, to break it up a bit, then whisk it into the egg-yolk mixture.

In a large, scrupulously clean bowl and using clean beaters, whisk the egg whites until they form stiff peaks. Add the remaining sugar to the egg whites, a quarter at a time, whisking after each addition.

Using a large metal spoon, carefully fold the melted chocolate mixture into the egg-yolk mixture. Finally, fold in the beaten egg whites. Be as gentle as you can so that you keep as much air in the mixture as possible.

Pour the mixture into the prepared pan and bake in the preheated oven for 40–45 minutes, or until well risen. Let cool in the pan. It will sink in the middle as it does so, but this is normal.

Transfer the pan to a large serving plate or board and release the side clip. Lift the ring from the torte and carefully slide the cake off the pan base, using a spatula or fish slice. Peel off the base paper. Dust the torte lightly with cocoa powder and scatter the chopped hazelnuts over the top.

apple, rum and raisin cupcakes

These are cupcakes with a difference — they contain all the flavours of a Caribbean rum punch: dark rum, spices and fruit.

100 g/⅔ cup raisins

2 tablespoons dark rum

150 g/10 tablespoons butter, softened and cubed

150 g/¾ cup light muscovado or packed light brown soft sugar

2 large eggs, lightly beaten

175 g/1⅓ cups self-raising flour, sifted

generous fresh grating of nutmeg

2 dessert apples

1 ripe banana

finely grated zest of 1 orange

Icing

75 g/½ cup icing/confectioners' sugar

½ teaspoon freshly grated nutmeg, plus extra for sprinkling

1 teaspoon dark rum

3–4 teaspoons freshly squeezed orange juice

a 12-hole muffin pan, lined with cupcake cases

Makes 12

Preheat the oven to 180°C (350°F) Gas 4.

Tip the raisins into a small bowl with the rum, stir and set aside while you make the rest of the mixture.

Put the butter, sugar, beaten eggs, flour and grated nutmeg in an electric mixer (or use a large mixing bowl and an electric whisk). Whisk together to combine.

Core, peel and chop the apples into small pieces. Peel and chop the banana into small pieces too and stir into the cake mixture with the apples, three-quarters of the orange zest and all the soaked raisins and rum.

Divide the mixture between the cupcake cases. Bake in the preheated oven for 25–30 minutes, or until risen and golden. Let cool on a wire rack.

When you are ready to ice the cupcakes, sift the icing/confectioners' sugar into a small bowl and stir in the grated nutmeg. Add the rum, then the orange juice, a teaspoon at a time, stirring between each addition — you may not need it all. Spoon the icing over the cupcakes and sprinkle a little extra nutmeg and the remaining grated orange zest over each one. Let set before serving.

brown sugar pavlova with cinnamon cream and pomegranate

This is a perfect winter party piece. In the summer, top the meringue with summer berries or a mixture of sliced peaches or nectarines and blueberries instead.

4 large egg whites

50 g/¼ cup packed light muscovado sugar

175 g/¾ cup (caster) sugar (unrefined is best here)

1 teaspoon cornflour/cornstarch

1 teaspoon white wine vinegar

300 ml/1¼ cups double/heavy or whipping cream

1 tablespoon icing/confectioners' sugar

1½ teaspoons ground cinnamon

150 g/1 cup pomegranate seeds

a baking sheet, lined with baking parchment (don't grease it, or your egg whites will collapse!)

Serves 8

Preheat the oven to 140°C (275°F) Gas 1.

Put the egg whites in a large, scrupulously clean bowl and whisk with an electric whisk (or use an electric mixer) until they form stiff peaks. Add the sugars, a tablespoon at a time, whisking constantly. Add the cornflour/cornstarch and vinegar with the final addition of sugar.

Pile the meringue mixture onto the prepared baking sheet and form into a circle about 22 cm/9 inches in diameter. Make swirls in the meringue with a skewer or the end of a teaspoon. Bake in the preheated oven for 1 hour, then turn the oven off and leave the pavlova in until cold – overnight is ideal.

To finish, whip the cream with the icing/confectioners' sugar and cinnamon to soft peaks. Pile it onto the pavlova and scatter the pomegranate seeds over the top.

index